PATHWAYS

Reading, Writing, and Critical Thinking

2A

Laurie Blass   Mari Vargo

NATIONAL
GEOGRAPHIC
LEARNING | HEINLE
CENGAGE Learning

Australia • Brazil • Japan • Korea • Mexico • Singapore • Spain • United Kingdom • United States

Pathways Split Text 2A
Reading, Writing, and Critical Thinking
Laurie Blass and Mari Vargo

Publisher: Andrew Robinson

Executive Editor: Sean Bermingham

Contributing Editors: Bernard Seal, Sylvia Bloch

Director of Global Marketing: Ian Martin

Marketing Manager: Caitlin Thomas

Director of Content and Media Production:
  Michael Burggren

Senior Content Project Manager: Daisy Sosa

Manufacturing Manager: Marcia Locke

Manufacturing Buyer: Marybeth Hennebury

Associate Manager, Operations:
  Leila Hishmeh

Cover Design: Page 2 LLC

Cover Image: Patrick McFeeley/
  National Geographic Image Collection

Interior Design: Page 2, LLC

Composition: Page 2, LLC

ISBN 13: 978-1-285-45252-4
ISBN 10: 1-285-45252-6

Cengage Learning Asia Pte Ltd
151 Lorong Chuan #02-08
New Tech Park
Singapore 556741

National Geographic Learning
20 Channel Center Street
Boston, MA 02210
USA

Cengage Learning is a leading provider of customized learning solutions with office locations around the globe, including Singapore, the United Kingdom, Australia, Mexico, Brazil, and Japan. Locate your local office at: **ngl.cengage.com**

Cengage Learning products are represented in Canada by Nelson Education, Ltd.

Visit National Geographic Learning online at **ngl.cengage.com**
Visit our website at **www.cengageasia.com**

Printed in Singapore
2 3 4 5 6 7 8 17 16 15 14

Contents

PLACES TO EXPLORE IN

▲ Tornado Alley in the U.S. has the world's most extreme weather. **page 125**

▲ Chichén Itzá in Mexico has been called one of the Seven Wonders of the World. **page 155**

▲ Barcelona's La Sagrada Família will finally be complete in 2026—more than 100 years after it began. **page 145**

Gold miners in Choco are using old mining methods with new innovations. **page 195**

PATHWAYS

3,500-year-old Göbekli Tepe in Turkey may be the oldest religious building in the world. **page 154**

▲ In Singapore, laws are strict and working hours are long. So why are Singaporeans so happy? **page 5**

What is the secret to long ▲ life? Ask the people of Japan's Okinawan islands. **page 9**

On the island of ▲ Vorovoro, Fiji, an online community has created its own tribe. **page 52**

A remarkable world exists beneath the waves of Australia's Coral Sea. **page 63**

Madagascar is home to some of the world's most poisonous species. **page 109**

Scope and Sequence

Unit	Academic Pathways	Vocabulary
 **1** **Happiness** *Page 1* **Academic Track:** Health Science	**Lesson A:** Identifying an author's main ideas Guessing meaning from context **Lesson B:** Understanding a classification text **Lesson C:** Introduction to the paragraph Writing a topic sentence	Understanding meaning from context Using new vocabulary in an everyday context **Word Partners:** *factor*
 **2** **Big Ideas** *Page 21* **Academic Track:** Interdisciplinary	**Lesson A:** Understanding a biographical text Identifying supporting ideas **Lesson B:** Ranking ideas in order of priority **Lesson C:** Supporting the main idea and giving details Writing a descriptive paragraph	Understanding meaning from context Identifying part of speech from context Using new vocabulary in an everyday context **Word Link:** *-tion, -able*
 **3** **Connected Lives** *Page 41* **Academic Track:** Anthropology/ Sociology	**Lesson A:** Skimming for gist Making inferences **Lesson B:** Reading a magazine article **Lesson C:** Writing a concluding sentence Writing an opinion paragraph	Understanding meaning from context Using new vocabulary in an everyday context **Word Link:** *-inter, -al* **Word Partners:** *environmentally*
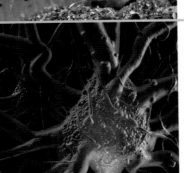 **4** **Deep Trouble** *Page 61* **Academic Track:** Interdisciplinary	**Lesson A:** Interpreting visual information Examining problems and solutions **Lesson B:** Understanding graphic information Reading an interview **Lesson C:** Explaining a chart or graph	Understanding meaning from context Using new vocabulary in an everyday context **Word Partners:** *reduce, informed* **Word Link:** *mini-*
5 **Memory and Learning** *Page 81* **Academic Track:** Health Science/ Psychology	**Lesson A:** Identifying cause and effect in an expository text **Lesson B:** Synthesizing information from multiple texts **Lesson C:** Using an outline to plan a paragraph Writing a paragraph with supporting information	Understanding meaning from context Using new vocabulary in an everyday context **Word Link:** *-ize, trans-* **Word Partners:** *stress*

Reading	Writing	Viewing	Critical Thinking
Interpreting infographics Predicting for main idea Understanding the gist Identifying key details Using clues in opening sentences **Skill Focus:** Identifying main ideas	**Goal:** Writing a paragraph **Grammar:** Using simple present tense **Skill:** Writing a topic sentence	**Video:** *Longevity Leaders* Guessing meaning from context Viewing for general understanding Viewing for specific information	Inferring word meaning from context Analyzing and discussing information Synthesizing information to identify similarities **CT Focus:** Inferring meaning from context
Interpreting survey information Predicting for main idea Understanding the gist Identifying key details **Skill Focus:** Identifying supporting ideas	**Goal:** Writing a descriptive paragraph **Grammar:** Using simple past tense **Skill:** Supporting the main idea and giving details	**Video:** *Solar Cooking* Viewing for general understanding Viewing for specific information	Identifying problems and solutions Synthesizing information to identify similarities Analyzing and ranking ideas and providing reasons **CT Focus:** Deciding on criteria for ranking
Interpreting maps and charts Predicting for main idea Understanding the gist Identifying key details Scanning for key details **Skill Focus:** Skimming for gist	**Goal:** Writing an opinion paragraph **Grammar:** Using present perfect tense **Skill:** Writing a concluding sentence	**Video:** *Lamu: Tradition and Modernity* Guessing meaning from context Viewing for general understanding Viewing for specific information	Synthesizing information to identify similarities Synthesizing information for group discussion Analyzing text for function and purpose **CT Focus:** Making inferences from a text
Interpreting maps Understanding the gist Identifying main ideas Identifying purpose Identifying key details **Skill Focus:** Interpreting visual information (graph/map)	**Goal:** Writing a paragraph that explains a chart or graph **Grammar:** Describing charts and graphs **Skill:** Explaining a chart or graph	**Video:** *Saving Bluefin Tuna* Viewing to confirm predictions Viewing for general understanding Viewing for specific information	Inferring word meaning from context Evaluating author arguments Synthesizing textual and visual information for discussion Analyzing text for key information **CT Focus:** Analyzing and evaluating problems and solutions presented in a text
Interpreting infographics Understanding the gist Identifying key details Classifying information using a T-chart Identifying main ideas **Skill Focus:** Identifying cause and effect	**Goal:** Writing a paragraph with supporting information **Grammar:** Using *by* + gerund **Skill:** Using an outline	**Video:** *Memory School* Viewing to confirm predictions Viewing for general understanding Viewing for specific information	Inferring author opinion from the text Synthesizing information for group discussion Analyzing text for function and purpose **CT Focus:** Applying a new method for internalization

EXPLORE A UNIT

Each unit has three lessons.

Lessons A and B develop academic reading skills and vocabulary by focusing on two aspects of the unit theme. A video section acts as a content bridge between Lessons A and B. The language and content in these sections provide the stimulus for a final writing task (Lesson C).

The **unit theme** focuses on an academic content area relevant to students' lives, such as Health Science, Business and Technology, and Environmental Science.

Academic Pathways

highlight the main academic skills of each lesson.

UNIT
4

Deep Trouble

ACADEMIC PATHWAYS
Lesson A: Interpreting visual information
Examining problems and solutions
Lesson B: Understanding graphic information
Reading an interview
Lesson C: Explaining a chart or graph

Think and Discuss

1. What ocean or sea is nearest your home? When was the last time you saw it?
2. Do you eat seafood? If yes, what types do you eat? If no, why not?

▲ A school of barracuda surrounds a diver off New Hanover Island, Papua New Guinea.

61

Exploring the Theme

provides a visual introduction to the unit. Learners are encouraged to think critically and share ideas about the unit topic.

Exploring the Theme

Look at the map and read the information. Then discuss the questions.

1. What do the colors of the map show? What kinds of "activity" does this refer to?
2. Which areas have the highest impact, or effect, of human activities?
3. How is human activity affecting, or changing, the four places described? How are the effects similar and different?

North Sea
Pollution from shipping, farming, and offshore drilling is causing "dead zones"—places without enough oxygen for plants and fish to live. Overfishing adds to the problem.

◄ Pollution from offshore oil and gas drilling is one cause of the North Sea's dead zones.

East China Sea
Several large rivers bring pollution into the sea. It is also a major fishing area and shipping route. Together, these factors cause serious problems for the ocean environment.

◄ Container ships are a common sight on the rivers that flow from several countries into the East China Sea.

Coral Sea
The Coral Sea has less impact from human activity than other oceans. However, the water is warming and becoming acidic.* Plants and fish cannot live in acidic water.

◄ The humphead wrasse is among thousands of fish species living in the Great Barrier Reef in Australia's Coral Sea.

Ocean Impact

Human activities are affecting, in some way, all of the world's oceans. These activities include fishing, farming, manufacturing, and offshore gas and oil drilling.

Impact of human activity
- Very high
- High
- Medium high
- Medium
- Low
- Very low

Caribbean Sea
Pollution and overfishing are causing some fish species to disappear. The temperature of the water is increasing, too. The rising water temperature makes it more difficult for species to survive.

◄ Garbage washes ashore on the southern edge of Aruba in the Caribbean.

◄ Most ocean waves expand carpet the ocean floor of Australia's Coral Sea.

*If something is **acidic**, it contains acid, a chemical that is harmful to the environment.

62 | UNIT 4

DEEP TROUBLE | 63

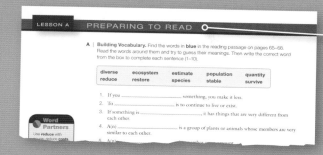

In **Preparing to Read**, learners are introduced to key vocabulary items from the reading passage. Lessons A and B each present and practice 10 target vocabulary items.

Reading A is a single, linear text related to the unit theme. Each reading passage is recorded on the audio program.

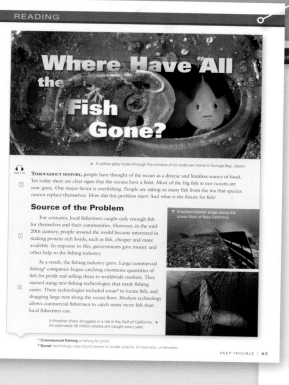

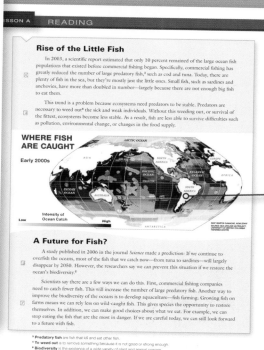

Maps and other graphic formats help to develop learners' visual literacy.

Guided comprehension tasks and reading strategy instruction enable learners to improve their academic literacy and critical thinking skills.

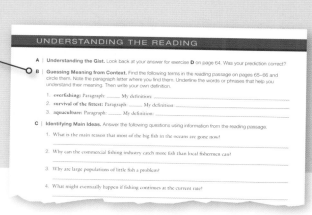

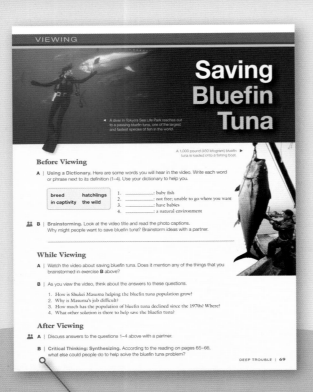

Saving Bluefin Tuna

◄ A diver in Tokyo's Sea Life Park reaches out to a passing bluefin tuna, one of the largest and fastest species of fish in the world.

A 1,000 pound (450 kilogram) bluefin ► tuna is loaded onto a fishing boat.

Before Viewing

A | **Using a Dictionary.** Here are some words you will hear in the video. Write each word or phrase next to its definition (1–4). Use your dictionary to help you.

| breed | hatchlings |
| in captivity | the wild |

1. _____: baby fish
2. _____: not free; unable to go where you want
3. _____: have babies
4. _____: a natural environment

B | **Brainstorming.** Look at the video title and read the photo captions. Why might people want to save bluefin tuna? Brainstorm ideas with a partner.

While Viewing

A | Watch the video about saving bluefin tuna. Does it mention any of the things that you brainstormed in exercise **B** above?

B | As you view the video, think about the answers to these questions.

1. How is Shukei Masuma helping the bluefin tuna population grow?
2. Why is Masuma's job difficult?
3. How much has the population of bluefin tuna declined since the 1970s? Where?
4. What other solution is there to help save the bluefin tuna?

After Viewing

A | Discuss answers to the questions 1–4 above with a partner.

B | **Critical Thinking: Synthesizing.** According to the reading on pages 65–66, what else could people do to help solve the bluefin tuna problem?

DEEP TROUBLE | 69

Viewing tasks related to an authentic National Geographic video serve as a content-bridge between Lessons A and B. (Video scripts are on pages 203–208.)

Learners need to use their **critical thinking skills** to relate video content to information in the previous reading.

Word Link and ***Word Partners*** boxes develop learners' awareness of word structure, collocations, and usage.

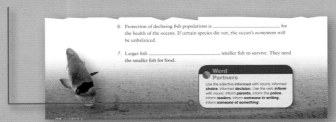

6. Protection of declining fish populations is _____ for the health of the oceans. If certain species die out, the ocean's ecosystem will be unbalanced.

7. Larger fish _____ smaller fish to survive. They need the smaller fish for food.

Word Partners

Use the adjective **informed** with nouns: informed **choice**, informed **decision**. Use the verb **inform** with nouns: inform **parents**, inform the **police**, inform **readers**, inform **someone in writing**, inform **someone of something**.

Guided pre-reading tasks and strategy tips encourage learners to think critically about what they are going to read.

C | **Brainstorming.** Note some ideas about things you can do to help keep the oceans healthy.

stop eating fish with declining populations,
_____
_____

Strategy

Use titles and visuals, such as charts and maps, to predict what a passage will be about.

D | **Predicting.** Look at the titles and visuals on pages 72–73. Then complete the sentences.

1. I think the interview is about a person who _____

LESSON B   READING

🎧 track 1-11

An Interview with Barton Seaver

[A] Barton Seaver is a chef and conservationist[1] who wants our help to save the oceans. He believes that the choices we make for dinner have a direct impact on the ocean's health. According to Seaver, individuals can make a big difference by making informed choices.

Q. *Should people stop eating seafood?*

[B] People should definitely not stop eating seafood altogether. There are certain species that have been severely overfished and that people should avoid for environmental reasons. But I believe that we can save the oceans while continuing to enjoy seafood. For example, some types of seafood, such as Alaskan salmon, come from well-managed fisheries. And others, such as farmed mussels and oysters, actually help to restore declining wild populations and clean up polluted waters.

Q. *What kind of seafood should people eat? What should they not eat?*

[C] My general advice is to eat fish and shellfish that are low on the food chain and that can be harvested[2] with minimal impact on the environment. Some examples include farmed mussels, clams and oysters, anchovies, sardines, and herring. People should not eat the bigger fish of the sea, like tuna, orange roughy, shark, sturgeon, and swordfish.

Q. *Why did you choose to dedicate[3] your life to the ocean:*

[D] I believe that the next great advance in human knowledge will come not from new discoveries, but rather from learning how we relate to our natural world. Humans are an essential part of nature, yet humans do not have a very strong relationship with the world around them. I have dedicated myself to helping people to understand our place on this planet through the foods that we eat.

Q. *Why do you believe people should care about the health of the oceans?*

[E] The health of the oceans is directly linked to the health of people. The ocean provides most of the air we breathe. It has a big effect on the weather that we rely on for crops and food production. It also provides a necessary and vital[4] diet for billions of people on the planet. So I don't usually say that I am trying to save the oceans. I prefer to say that I am trying to save the vital things that we rely on the ocean for.

[1] A **conservationist** is someone who works to protect the environment.
[2] When you **harvest** something, such as a crop or other type of food, you gather it in.
[3] When you **dedicate** yourself to something, you give it a lot of time and effort because you think it is important.
[4] Something that is **vital** is very important.

72 | UNIT 4

Lesson B's reading passage

presents a further aspect of the unit theme, using a variety of text types and graphic formats.

Critical thinking tasks require

learners to analyze, synthesize, and critically evaluate ideas and information in each reading.

3. Eating a pound of orange roughy is like eating _____ of shrimp.

4. Barton Seaver says he works to protect the oceans because _____

CT Focus
Examine the problems and solutions in exercise **D**. Do you think each suggestion is an effective solution to each problem? Are the suggestions realistic?

D | Critical Thinking: Analyzing Problems and Solutions. For each problem below, write one or two of Barton Seaver's suggestions that might help solve it.

Problems	Suggestions
Some wild fish populations are declining.	
People don't have a strong relationship with the world around them.	

E | Critical Thinking: Synthesizing. Discuss the questions in small groups.

1. Barton Seaver recommends that people eat smaller fish. How can this help the ocean's ecosystem?

2. Do you agree with Seaver that "humans do not have a very strong relationship with the world around them"? What are some examples in this unit for or against this idea?

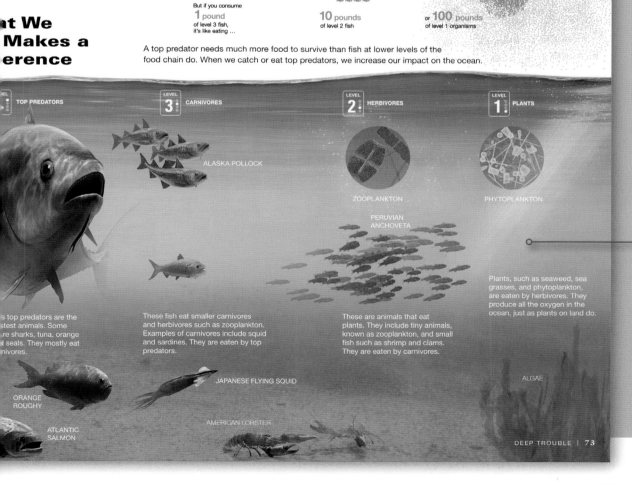

LEVEL 4 TOP PREDATORS
When you eat
1 pound
of a level 4 fish,
it's like eating ...

LEVEL 3 CARNIVORES
10 pounds of level 3 fish

LEVEL 2 HERBIVORES
or **100 pounds**
of level 2 fish

LEVEL 1 PLANTS
or **1,000 pounds**
of level 1 organisms

But if you consume
1 pound
of level 3 fish,
it's like eating ...

10 pounds
of level 2 fish

or **100 pounds**
of level 1 organisms

A top predator needs much more food to survive than fish at lower levels of the food chain do. When we catch or eat top predators, we increase our impact on the ocean.

t We Makes a erence

Authentic charts and graphics

from National Geographic support the main text, helping learners comprehend key ideas.

ALASKA POLLOCK

ZOOPLANKTON

PHYTOPLANKTON

PERUVIAN ANCHOVETA

Plants, such as seaweed, sea grasses, and phytoplankton, are eaten by herbivores. They produce all the oxygen in the ocean, just as plants on land do.

s top predators are the stest animals. Some re sharks, tuna, orange d seals. They mostly eat nivores.

These fish eat smaller carnivores and herbivores such as zooplankton. Examples of carnivores include squid and sardines. They are eaten by top predators.

These are animals that eat plants. They include tiny animals, known as zooplankton, and small fish such as shrimp and clams. They are eaten by carnivores.

JAPANESE FLYING SQUID

ORANGE ROUGHY

ATLANTIC SALMON

AMERICAN LOBSTER

ALGAE

The **Goal of Lesson C** is for learners to relate their own views and experience to the theme of the unit by completing a guided writing assignment.

Integrated **grammar practice and writing skill development** provides scaffolding for the writing assignment.

The **Independent Student Handbook** provides further language support and self-study strategies for independent learning.
▶ see pages 209–217.

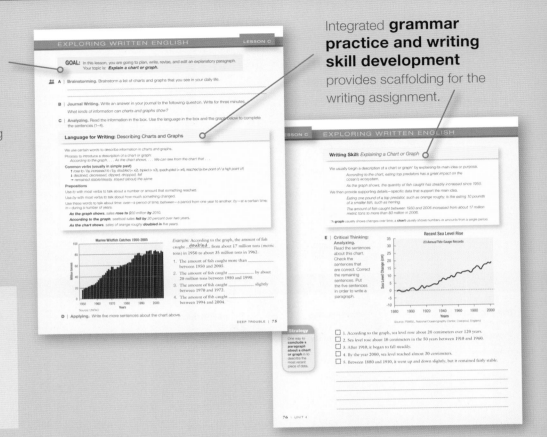

Resources for *Pathways* Level 2

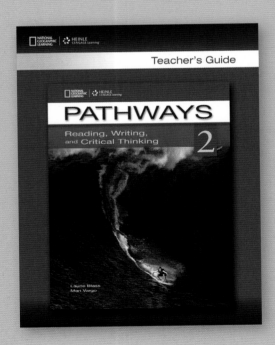

Teacher's Guide including teacher's notes, expansion activities, rubrics for evaluating written assignments, and answer keys for activities in the Student Book.

Video DVD with authentic National Geographic clips relating to each of the 10 units.

Audio CDs with audio recordings of the Student Book reading passages.

A **guided process approach** develops learners' confidence in planning, drafting, revising, and editing their written work.

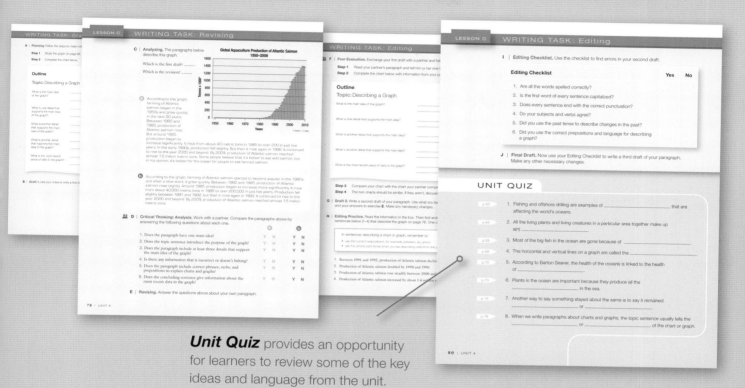

Unit Quiz provides an opportunity for learners to review some of the key ideas and language from the unit.

Assessment CD-ROM with ExamView®

containing a bank of ready-made questions for quick and effective assessment.

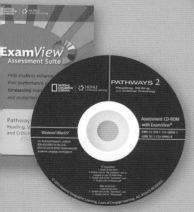

Online Workbook, powered by MyELT,

with both teacher-led and self-study options. This contains the 10 National Geographic video clips, supported by interactive, automatically graded activities that practice the skills learned in the Student Books.

Classroom Presentation Tool CD-ROM featuring audio and video

clips, and interactive activities from the Student Book. These can be used with an interactive whiteboard or computer projector.

Credits

Text

4-5, 12-13: Adapted from "Thrive: Finding Happiness the Blue Zones Way," by Dan Buettner: National Geographic Books, 2011, **25-26:** Adapted from "Windmills of His Mind," by Karen Lange: http://blogs.ngm.com/blog_central/2009/10/the-windmills-of-his-mind.html, October 2009, **32-33:** Adapted from "Big Ideas, Little Packages": NGM November 2010, and "Hayat Sindi": http://www.nationalgeographic.com/explorers/bios/hayat-sindi/, **45-46:** Adapted from "Michael Wesch": http://www.nationalgeographic.com/explorers/bios/michael-wesch/, **52-53:** Adapted from "Welcome to Internet Island," by James Vlahos: National Geographic Adventure, February 2007, **65-66:** Adapted from "Overfishing": http://ocean.nationalgeographic.com/ocean/critical-issues-overfishing/, **72-73:** Adapted from "Seafood Crisis," by Paul Greenberg: NGM October 2010, **85-86:** Adapted from "Remember This," by Joshua Foer: NGM November 2007, **92:** Adapted from "Memory Boosters: How to Help": NGM November 2007, **93:** Adapted from "Direct Evidence of the Role of Sleep in Memory Formation Uncovered," by David Braun: http://blogs.nationalgeographic.com/blogs/news/chiefeditor/2009/09/sleep-and-memory.html

NGM = National Geographic Magazine

Photo Images

Cover: Patrick McFeeley/National Geographic, **IFC:** Katie Stoops, **IFC:** Michael Wesch, **IFC:** Courtesy of Dan Buettner, **IFC:** Tyrone Turner/National Geographic, **IFC:** Kris Krug, **IFC:** Jim Webb, **IFC:** Embrace Global, **IFC:** Rebecca Hale/National Geographic, **IFC:** Bedford, James/National Geographic Stock, **IFC:** Moving Windmills Project, Inc., **i:** Wes. C. Skiles/National Geographic, **iii:** Steve Raymer/National Geographic, **iii:** Ken Eward/National Geographic Stock, **iii:** Lynsey Addario/National Geographic, **iii:** David Doubilet/National Geographic, **iii:** Gerd Ludwig/National Geographic Stock, **iii:** Bruce Dale/National Geographic Image Collection, **iii:** Mark Thiessen/National Geographic, **iii:** Simon Norfolk/National Geographic, **iii:** Joe Petersburger/National Geographic, **iii:** Ken Banks, kiwanja.net, **iv:** Campo, Colorado/National Geographic, **iv:** Simon Norfolk/National Geographic, **iv:** Stephen Chao/National Geographic, **iv:** Frans Lanting/National Geographic, **iv-v:** NASA Goddard Space Flight Center Image by Reto Stöckli (land surface, shallow water, clouds), **v:** ©2011/Vincent J. Musi/National Geographic Image Collection, **v:** Steve Raymer/National Geographic, **v:** David McLain/National Geographic, **v:** Ben Keene, **v:** David Doubilet/National Geographic, **v:** Joel Sartore/National Geographic, **vi:** Michael S. Lewis/National Geographic, **vi:** Moving Windmills Project, Inc., **vi:** Bobby Haas/National Geographic, **vi:** Brian J. Skerry/National Geographic, **vi:** Anne Keiser/National Geographic, **1:** Joel Sartore/National Geographic, **2-3:** Steve Raymer/National Geographic, **5:** Steve Raymer/National Geographic, **6:** Michael S. Lewis/National Geographic, **8:** Stephen St. John/National Geographic, **9:** David McLain/National Geographic Stock, **12:** Sisse Brimberg/National Geographic, **12:** David McLain/National Geographic, **12:** Lynsey Addario/National Geographic, **13:** Image courtesy of Dan Buettner, **21:** Ken Eward/National Geographic Stock, **22:** Ira Block/National Geographic, **23:** Wright, Orville/National Geographic, **23:** Paul Sutherland/National Geographic, **25:** Workshop Loves You, **26:** Moving Windmills Project, Inc., **26:** The Toronto Star/ZUMApress.com, **27:** Workshop Loves You, **28:** SuperStock/Corbis, **29:** Rebecca Hale/National Geographic, **29:** Jodi Cobb/National Geographic, **30:** Michael Melford/National Geographic Image Collection, **32:** Embrace Global, **32:** Rebecca Hale/National Geographic, **32:** Renee Comet/National Geographic, **33:** Kris Krug, **33:** Renee Comet/National Geographic, **41:** Susan Seubert/National Geographic, **43:** Lynsey Addario/National Geographic, **45:** Gerd Ludwig/National Geographic, **46:** Peter Essick/National Geographic, **46:** Michael Wesch, **49:** Bobby Haas/National Geographic, **50:** Ben Keene, **52:** James Vlahos, **52:** Ben Keene, **53:** James Vlahos, **53:** James Vlahos, **61:** David Doubilet/National Geographic, **62:** Hannele Lahti/National Geographic, **62-63:** Jason Edwards/National Geographic **63:** George Steinmetz/National Geographic, **63:** Paul Chesley/National Geographic, **63:** David Doubilet/National Geographic, **65:** Brian J. Skerry/National Geographic, **65:** Brian J. Skerry/National Geographic, **65:** Brian J. Skerry/National Geographic, **69:** Anderson, John (California)/National Geographic, **69:** David Doubilet/National Geographic, **70:** David Doubilet/National Geographic, **70-71:** Jason Edwards/National Geographic, **72:** Katie Stoops, **81:** Rebecca Hale/National Geographic, **82-83:** Maggie Steber/National Geographic, **83:** Anne Keiser/National Geographic, **85:** Gerd Ludwig/National Geographic Stock, **85:** The Granger Collection, NYC, **86:** Getty Images, **86:** David Alan Harvey/National Geographic, **88:** Steve and Donna O'Meara/National Geographic, **89:** Annie Griffiths/National Geographic, **92:** Justin Guariglia/National Geographic, **92:** PinonRoad/iStockphoto, **92:** Lisovskaya Natalia/Shutterstock, **93:** Courtesy of Dr. Arthur W. Toga, Laboratory of Neuro Imaging at UCLA, **100:** Syakobchuk Vasyl, 2009/Used under license from Shutterstock.com, **209:** David Doubilet/National Geographic

continued on p. 223

Happiness

ACADEMIC PATHWAYS

Lesson A: Identifying an author's main ideas
Guessing meaning from context
Lesson B: Understanding a classification text
Lesson C: Introduction to the paragraph
Writing a topic sentence

Think and Discuss

1. What does it mean to be happy?
2. Think of someone you know who seems happy.
How do you know he or she is happy?
Describe the person.

▲ A zebra butterfly brings joy to a young girl in Lincoln, Nebraska.

1

Exploring the Theme

Look at the information about two surveys and discuss the questions.

1. Where are the happiest places on Earth, according to the two surveys? How do the results compare?

2. Why do you think people from these countries are happy?

3. Imagine you want to find the happiest place in your country. What information would you look at? What questions would you ask?

World Happiness Survey ①

Happy Hot Spots

The **World Database of Happiness** brings together scientific reports on happiness from 149 countries around the world. The researchers ask people to rate their enjoyment of life on a scale from 0 to 10. The top six happiest nations according to the survey (2000–2009) are listed below. The happiest Asian country, Singapore, is 37th in the list; Malawi (62nd) is Africa's happiest nation. The world's richest nation, the United States, placed 21st.

❸ Iceland
Rating **8.2**
Pop.: 311,000
GDP pc: $38,300
Avg. Life: 80.9 years

❺ Finland
Rating **7.9**
Pop.: 5.3 million
GDP pc: $35,400
Avg. Life: 79.27 years

❷ Denmark
Rating **8.3**
Pop.: 5.5 million
GDP pc: $36,600
Avg. Life: 78.63 years

❻ Mexico
Rating **7.9**
Pop.: 113.7 million
GDP pc: $13,900
Avg. Life: 76.47 years

❶ Costa Rica
Rating **8.5**
Pop.: 4.6 million
GDP pc: $11,300
Avg. Life: 77.72 years

❹ Switzerland
Rating **8.0**
Pop.: 7.6 million
GDP pc: $42,600
Avg. Life: 81.07 years

Pop.: Population; **GDP pc:** Gross Domestic Product per capita (the value of goods and services produced by a country, divided by the number of people); **Avg. Life:** Average life expectancy.

Source: http://worlddatabaseofhappiness.eur.nl/

Happy Planet

The **Happy Planet Index** was started in 2006 by the New Economics Foundation (NEF). It measures average personal happiness together with a country's average life expectancy and environmental impact. The highest-rated countries have happy, long-living people without harming the environment.

The top six countries in the 2009 Index are listed below. Other countries in the top 20 include Brazil (9th), Egypt (12th), Saudi Arabia (13th), the Philippines (14th), Argentina (15th), and China (20th).

1 Costa Rica

2 Dominican Republic

3 Jamaica

4 Guatemala

5 Vietnam

6 Colombia

Source: http://www.happyplanetindex.org/

▲ An elderly Vietnamese woman smiles for a photo. Vietnam was rated #5 in the 2009 **Happy Planet Index**, the highest-placed Asian nation in that survey.

A | Building Vocabulary. Find the words in **blue** in the reading passage on pages 5–6. Read the words around them and try to guess their meanings. Then write the correct word or phrase from the box to complete each sentence (1–10).

access	basic necessities	confident	financial	freedom
poverty	provides	secure	socialize	standard of living

1. When you _____socialize_____, you spend time with other people for fun.
2. A country with a lot of _____poverty_____ has a lot of people who don't have money.
3. If you have _____access_____ to something, you can use it.
4. If you have complete _____freedom_____, you can do anything you want to do.
5. If a government _____provides_____ jobs to people, it gives jobs to people.
6. If you have a high _____standard of living_____, you are very comfortable and wealthy.
7. If you discuss your _____financial_____ situation, you are talking about money.
8. If you are _____secure_____, you feel safe and are not worried about anything.
9. If you have the _____basic necessities_____, you have a home and enough food to eat.
10. If you are _____confident_____ about something, you are sure about it.

B | Using Vocabulary. Answer the questions. Share your ideas with a partner.

1. What do you think are the **basic necessities** in life, besides food and a home?
2. Do you feel **confident** about your future? Why, or why not?
3. Who do you **socialize** with?

C | Brainstorming. List six things you think a person needs in order to be happy. Share your ideas with a partner.

1. _____   3. _____   5. _____

2. _____   4. _____   6. _____

Strategy

Read titles and subheads to predict what a passage is about. This will help you know what to expect as you read.

D | Predicting. Read the title and the subheads of the reading passage on pages 5–6. What do you think the reading passage is about?

a. Different things make different people happy.
b. Security is the most important thing for happiness.
c. Everyone needs the same basic things to be happy.

Word Link

To increase your vocabulary, use a dictionary to find other forms of a word, e.g., (adj.) confident, (n.) confidence; (adj.) secure, (n.) security; (n.) freedom, (adj.) free; (v.) socialize, (adj.) social; (adj.) financial, (n.) finance.

Is there a Recipe for Happiness?

▲ A happy street seller shows off his fruit selection at an open-air market in Singapore.

track 1-01

A **WHAT MAKES US HAPPY?** Money? Friends? A good job? Are the answers the same for everyone? According to world surveys, Mexico and Singapore are two happy countries—but their people may be happy for different reasons.

Safety and Security

B There are more than 19,000 people per square mile[1] in the small nation of Singapore. People on the island work an average of 70 hours per week. The country has strict laws, for example, against littering,[2] graffiti,[3] and even for not flushing a toilet. But according to the World Database of Happiness, Singapore is the happiest country in Asia. Why?

C One reason for Singapore's happiness is that the government provides the basic necessities, such as jobs and housing. There is almost no poverty, and Singapore has one of the lowest levels of unemployment in the world. The government creates jobs for people who are unemployed. It "tops up"[4] poorer people's income so everyone can have a minimum standard of living. The government also offers tax breaks[5] to people who look after their aging parents. This may be why 84 percent of older people live with their children. The result is a lot of closely connected families with roughly equal standards of living.

D People may not all be happy about the laws, but they are generally happy with the results—they don't step in litter, the public toilets work, and the streets are safe and clean. So for Singaporeans, it seems that living in a secure, clean, and safe place may be more important than having a lot of personal freedom. As Dr. Tan Ern Ser of Singapore's Institute of Policy Studies explains, "If you are hopeful and confident of getting what you want in life, then you are happy."

[1] A **square mile** = 2.59 square kilometers
[2] **Littering** is leaving garbage or trash lying around outside.
[3] **Graffiti** is words or pictures that are written or drawn on walls or other public places.
[4] If you **top** something **up**, you add to it to make it full.
[5] If the government gives someone a **tax break**, it lowers the amount of tax they have to pay.

Friends and Neighbors

E In many ways, Mexico is the opposite of Singapore. There are some parts of Mexico where people do not have a safe or secure life. Many people do not have jobs, enough food, or access to education. But, as in Singapore, most people in Mexico feel that they are happy. Why?

F One reason is the importance of socializing. According to psychologists, much of our happiness comes from remembering the small joys that happen throughout the day. Simple acts of socializing, such as talking with a neighbor or having dinner with friends, can greatly increase our overall happiness. People in Mexico socialize with family and friends a lot, and this adds to their happiness.

G But what about poverty? In Mexico, about half of the population is poor. However, most people in Mexico live near people in a similar financial

▲ About 60 percent of Mexico's population rates itself as "very happy"— about 24 percent more than Mexico's richer neighbor, the United States.

situation. If your neighbor doesn't have expensive items, such as a big house or an expensive car, you don't feel the need to have those things. So money, by itself, may not be so important for happiness. What matters more is how much money you have compared to the people around you.

A Mixed Recipe?

H So the question "What makes people happy?" does not seem to have a simple answer. Work, security, safety, freedom, and socializing with friends and family can all play important roles. As the examples of Singapore and Mexico suggest, there may be no single recipe for happiness. The good news is that we can each find our own.

Adapted from *Thrive: Finding Happiness the Blue Zones Way* by Dan Buettner, 2010

A | **Understanding the Gist.** Look back at your answer for exercise **D** on p. 4. Was your prediction correct?

B | **Identifying Key Details.** Match each statement (1–7) to the place it describes, according to the reading.

1. Most people here feel that they are happy.
2. Most people have equal standards of living.
3. The government provides the basic necessities.
4. Family is important to people.
5. People spend a lot of time with family.
6. People feel safe and secure.
7. Although many people are poor, most of them are happy.

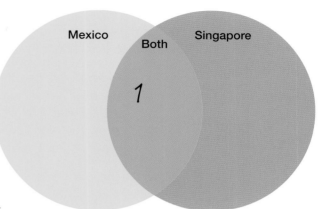

Mexico   Both   Singapore

1

C | **Critical Thinking: Guessing Meaning from Context.** Find and underline these **bold** words in the reading on page 5. Use context to identify their meaning. Then match the sentence halves to make definitions.

1. ____ If you are **strict**,
2. ____ If you are **flushing** something,
3. ____ If you are **unemployed**,
4. ____ If you **look after** people,
5. ____ If you make something **public**,

a. you provide it to everyone.
b. you take care of them and make sure they are well.
c. you don't allow people to behave badly.
d. you do not have a job.
e. you are cleaning or emptying it with a fast flow of water.

CT Focus

Use the context—the words around a word—to guess the meaning of a word you don't know. The context can also help you decide the word's part of speech, e.g., noun, verb, adjective, etc.

D | **Critical Thinking: Analyzing.** Discuss your answers to these questions with a partner.

1. Most people in Singapore have financial security and many people in Mexico do not. In what way is their financial situation similar?
2. According to the author, socializing can make people happy. What examples does he give? Do you agree with his view?

E | **Personalizing.** Complete the sentences with your own ideas.

1. I think (*safety and security / personal freedom / socializing*) is most important for happiness.
2. I usually socialize about _____ hours a week, and I (*work / study*) about _____ hours a week.
3. I think I would prefer to live in (*Singapore / Mexico*) because _____
_____.

Reading Skill: *Identifying the Main Idea*

The main idea of a paragraph is the most important idea, or the idea that the paragraph is about. A good paragraph has one main idea and one or more supporting ideas. Read the paragraph below and think about the main idea.

> *Researchers have found that the sunny weather in Mexico is one of the reasons that people there are happy. Mexico has many hours of sunlight, so people in Mexico get a lot of vitamin D. Vitamin D is important for overall health and well-being. Also, studies show that when people tan, they make more endorphins—chemicals in our bodies that make us feel happy.*

Which of these statements is the main idea of the paragraph?

> *a. People in Mexico are happy because they get a lot of vitamin D.*
>
> *b. Tanning makes us create more endorphins, which make us feel happy.*
>
> *c. Mexico gets a lot of sun, which may make people there happier.*

The last sentence is the main idea. The other two sentences are supporting ideas that explain the main idea.

A | **Matching.** Look back at the reading on pages 5–6. Match each main idea below to a paragraph from the reading (**A–H**).

_____ C 1. One reason that people are happy is the government takes care of them financially.

_____ F 2. Socializing is important because it can contribute a lot to happiness.

_____ d 3. You do not need to have a lot of money to be happy.

_____ H 4. There are different answers to the question "What makes people happy?"

track **1-02**

B | **Identifying the Main Idea.** Read the information about Denmark. Then write the main idea of the paragraph.

It's hard to be happy when you're unhealthy. According to the World Database of Happiness, Denmark is the second happiest country in the world, and most Danes are fit. They have a lower rate of obesity than many of their European neighbors. Danish cities are designed so it's easy to walk or bike from one place to another. With a 30-minute walk, you can go from the city of Copenhagen to the ocean, where you can sail or swim, or to the woods, where you can hike. Everyone has easy access to recreation.

Main Idea: _____

_____

Roads in Copenhagen have a special lane just for cyclists. ▲

Longevity Leaders

Before Viewing

▲ Not many people live to be 100 years old or older. But there are some places in the world where people—such as this Sardinian farmer—live very long, healthy lives.

A | **Guessing Meaning from Context.** You will hear the words and phrases in **bold** in the video. Discuss the meaning of each one with a partner. Write definitions for the words and phrases.

1. Some countries have a lot of **centenarians**. These people live to be 100 years old or older.
2. Dan Buettner wanted to learn the secret of **longevity**. He wanted to know why people in some countries live a very long time.
3. Some young people eat a lot of **processed foods**, such as frozen pizza and soft drinks. These kinds of food often aren't good for you. Natural foods are usually healthier.
4. Many older people have a **traditional lifestyle**. They do things the same way that people have done for a long time.
5. Some older people spend time with friends, exercise, and play games. They like to stay **active**.

B | **Brainstorming.** What kinds of things do you think centenarians do to stay healthy?

____eat well____   _____   _____   _____

While Viewing

A | Watch the video about places where people live a long time. Does it mention any of the things that you listed in exercise **B** above? Circle any items that are mentioned.

B | As you view the video, think about the answers to these questions.

1. How many people are alive in the world now? How many will there be by the middle of the century?
2. Why are there more elderly people now than there were before?
3. What kinds of traditional lifestyles are disappearing? Why? What will happen if they continue to disappear?

After Viewing

A | Discuss answers to the questions 1–3 above with a partner.

B | **Critical Thinking: Synthesizing.** What do the centenarians in the video and the people in Singapore and Mexico have in common?

A | **Building Vocabulary.** Find the words or forms of the words in **bold** in the reading passage on pages 12–13. Look at the words around the bold words to guess their meanings. Then circle the best definition (**a** or **b**) of each word.

1. A **researcher** who studies happiness might ask people what kinds of things make them happy.

   a. someone who studies something and tries to discover facts about it
   b. someone who teaches subjects such as science and math in school

2. A person's **long-term** goals can include going to college and then medical school.

   a. happening over a long time
   b. traveling for a long distance

3. It's important to live in a **community** that you like. Do you like the people who live near you? Does the area have good places to shop, eat, and socialize?

   a. the place where you live
   b. a place where people meet

4. Most happy people have a **hobby**, such as writing, surfing, or painting.

   a. something that you do for money, such as a job
   b. an activity that you enjoy doing in your free time

CT Focus

Look for key words to help you guess meaning from context, e.g., *help others, no money, work.*

5. Some people **volunteer** to help others who are in need. Although you may get no money for volunteering, the work can make you feel good about yourself.

   a. do something without being paid
   b. go to school with a group of people

6. People feel happier when they are **grateful** for the things that they have. They spend less time wanting things that they don't have.

   a. thankful   b. excited

7. A person's **mood** can depend on many things. For example, if someone says something nice about you, it can make you feel good.

   a. the place where you spend most of your time
   b. the way you feel at a particular time

8. Healthy food, exercise, and friends are important for a person's **well-being**.

   a. health and happiness
   b. the way you spend your time

9. In many countries, adult children **support** their elderly parents. The children pay their parents' bills and provide them with food and a place to live.

   a. help   b. teach

Word Partners

Use **factor** with:
(*adj.*) **contributing** factor, **deciding** factor, **important** factor, **key** factor; (*n.*) **risk** factor.

10. Good health is one **factor** that can make you a happy person. A close group of friends is another factor.

   a. one of the things that causes a situation
   b. something that is difficult or causes problems

B | Using Vocabulary. Answer the questions in complete sentences. Then share your sentences with a partner.

1. What are some of your **long-term** goals?

   Marry

2. What kinds of opportunities do you have to socialize in your **community**?

   political

3. What is your favorite **hobby**?

   Games , sports

4. What are you **grateful** for in your life?

   Family

C | Predicting. Look at the title, subheads, and opening paragraph on pages 12–13. What do you think is the gist of the reading?

a. Your community is the most important factor for your happiness.

b. Self, home, and financial life are more important for happiness than social life, workplace, or community.

c. There are some small changes you can make in your life to increase your happiness.

D | Brainstorming. The reading looks at six factors related to happiness. Write the factors in the word web below. Then, with a partner, brainstorm some words that you think might relate to each one.

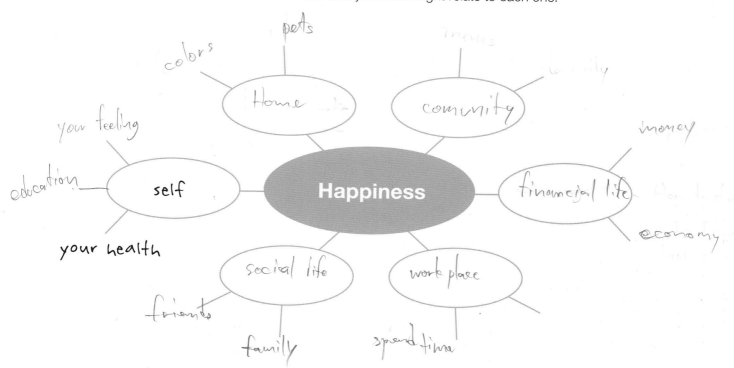

Six Keys to Happiness

track 1-03

▲ **Copenhagen, Denmark**. According to a global survey, Danish people are among the world's happiest people, second to Costa Ricans.

A RESEARCHERS HAVE FOUND that different people need different things to be happy. But there are some basic things that you can do to become happier. According to researcher Dan Buettner, the way to have long-term happiness is to make changes in six areas of our lives: Self, Home, Financial Life, Social Life, Workplace, and Community.

Self

B Your self includes your education, your health, and your sense of purpose—the feeling that you are doing something important. It's important to take care of yourself and to connect with the people around you. First, find a hobby. This gives you a chance to spend time focusing on your interests and talents and to meet people with similar interests. Denmark is one of the happiest countries on Earth, and 95 percent of Danes belong to clubs. You can also volunteer. Volunteering takes the focus off your own problems and makes you feel grateful for what you have.

Home

C How you arrange your home can make you happier. Create a quiet, dark area where you can sit and relax. Paint your living room yellow—it can increase energy and improve mood. It also helps to own a pet. Pets can increase their owners' self-esteem,[1] make them feel calm, and provide love and friendship.

COMMUNITY

SELF

◀ **Okinawa, Japan.** Close families and friendships help make Okinawa one of the longest-living and happiest places on the planet.

▼ **Paro, Bhutan.** Four rice farmers take a lunch break in Bhutan, a country famous for its GNH, or "Gross National Happiness."

Financial Life

D This is the way you think about and spend money. According to Ed Diener, author of *Happiness: Unlocking the Mysteries of Psychological Wealth*, the key to greater well-being is to have money, but not to want it too much. Try to spend money on things that give you long-lasting pleasure. Try not to waste money. Buy things that will really enrich your life, such as music lessons and dinners with friends and family.

Social Life

E It's important to have a good group of friends and people you see or communicate with regularly. Have friends that encourage you to eat right, to be active, to laugh, and to do your best. Researchers have found that having a close, happy friend can raise a person's mood by nine percent, while each unhappy friend lowers it by seven percent. Create a special group of friends—what Okinawans call a *moai*. Meet with them regularly and share with them when you have more of something than you need. Support each other in difficult times.

Workplace

F Your office, or wherever you spend your working hours, is a big part of your life. So it should be a place that you like. Find a job with people that you enjoy being around. That includes your boss. You don't want to spend 40 hours a week with people that you dislike. And do something that you feel strongly about. That's more important than a big salary.[2]

▲ Nicoya, Costa Rica. Costa Ricans, such as centenarian Francesca Castillo (pictured with author Dan Buettner), may be the world's happiest people.

Community

G The place where you live is probably more important than any other factor, including income, education, and religion. If possible, live near people who have about the same amount of money as you. Financial equality with your neighbors makes you less aware of what you don't have. Live in a neighborhood where you feel safe and where you can walk a lot. Walking makes you healthier, and healthier people are happier people.

[1] Your **self-esteem** is how you feel about yourself.
[2] A **salary** is the money that someone receives each month or year from their employer.

Adapted from *Thrive: Finding Happiness the Blue Zones Way* by Dan Buettner, 2010

A | **Understanding the Gist.** Look back at your answer for exercise **C** on page 11. Was your prediction correct?

B | **Identifying Main Ideas.** Read the statements below. Circle the main idea in each pair of statements (**a** or **b**).

Strategy

Look for **clues to the main idea** in the first (and sometimes second) sentence of a paragraph.

Self	a. You need to take care of yourself and connect with the people around you. b. Focus on your interests and talents and meet people who are like you.
Home	a. It's a good idea to paint your living room yellow. b. You should arrange your home so that it makes you feel happy.
Financial Life	a. You can be happy if you have enough money, but don't want money too much. b. If you waste money on things you don't need, you won't have enough money for things that you do need.
Social Life	a. A good group of friends can increase your happiness. b. Researchers say that a happy friend can increase our mood by nine percent.
Workplace	a. You spend a lot of time at work, so you should like your workplace. b. Your boss needs to be someone you enjoy working for.
Community	a. The place where you live is more important for happiness than anything else. b. Live around people who have the same amount of money as you do.

C | **Identifying Key Details.** Complete the following sentences about *"Six Keys to Happiness"*.

1. Volunteering can increase your happiness because _____
   _____

2. You should have friends who help you _____
   _____

3. People are less aware of what they don't have if they have _____
   _____

D | **Personalizing.** How can you improve each area of your life to become happier? Complete the notes using information from the reading or your own ideas. Write a sentence for each one.

Example: *I can take a painting class.*

Self _____
Home _____
Financial Life _____
Social Life _____
Workplace _____
Community _____

E | **Critical Thinking: Synthesizing.** Discuss the questions in small groups.

1. Which of the tips on pages 12–13 do you think the people in Mexico, Singapore, Sardinia, and Okinawa follow?

2. Can you think of other factors affecting happiness that are not mentioned in the reading passages and video?

GOAL: In this lesson, you are going to plan, write, revise, and edit a paragraph. Your topic is:

Do you think people in your community are generally happy or unhappy?

A | **Brainstorming.** Brainstorm a list of things that make people in your community happy and a list of things that people in your community may be unhappy about.

	Time	
hobby		work hand
Nature	life	city life
basic nessaties	Money	popordie
Comfortable	sete	un comfortable

Strategy

When you **brainstorm**, think of as many ideas as possible related to your topic. Don't worry about whether the ideas are good or bad—write down all the ideas you can think of.

B | **Journal Writing.** Use your ideas from exercise **A** to write a response in your journal to the following question. Write for three minutes.

Are the people in your community generally happy or unhappy?

C | Read the information in the box. Use the present tense of the verbs in parentheses to complete the sentences (1–5).

Language for Writing: *Review of the Simple Present*

We use the simple present to talk about facts or things that are generally true.

> *About 5.1 million people **live** in Singapore.*
> *Singapore **doesn't have** a high unemployment rate.*

We also use the simple present to talk about habits and routines.

> *I **spend** two hours with my friends on most days.*
> *I **don't see** my friends on Sundays.*

For more explanation and examples, see page 214.

Example: Mike _____ loves _____ (love) his job.

1. Kim _____ has _____ (have) a great job.

2. We _____ see _____ (see) our friends three or four times a week.

3. My boss and my coworkers _____ are _____ (be) really friendly.

4. My family and I _____ don't feel _____ (not / feel) safe in our neighborhood.

5. We _____ don't like _____ (not / like) the city that we live in.

D | **Applying.** Write five sentences using the simple present tense. Write about things you do every day that make you feel happy.

Writing Skill: *Writing a Topic Sentence*

A paragraph is a group of sentences about one topic. Most paragraphs include a sentence that states the main idea of the paragraph. This sentence is called the topic sentence. Paragraphs often begin with topic sentences, but topic sentences can occur anywhere in a paragraph.

A topic sentence should introduce the main idea that the paragraph will discuss or examine.

Below are some examples of strong and weak topic sentences.

Strong Topic Sentences

> *One reason that Singaporeans are happy is that the government provides the basic necessities, such as jobs and housing.*

> *People in Mexico socialize a lot, and this may contribute to their happiness.*

Weak Topic Sentences

> *Singaporeans are happy.*

(If the paragraph is about the ways that the government improves people's happiness, this idea should be included in the topic sentence.)

> *People in Mexico socialize a lot.*

(If the paragraph is about how socializing contributes to people's happiness in Mexico, this idea should be included in the topic sentence.)

E | Identifying Topic Sentences. Underline the topic sentence in each paragraph. One of the topic sentences is stronger than the others.

1. In Mexico, family is important. Family members provide support to each other during difficult times. Grandmothers take care of grandchildren so the children's mothers can go to work and earn money. When they grow up, children take care of their parents. People in Mexico are generally happy as long as family members are close.

2. Studies have shown that laughter may be an important factor for our happiness, and people who laugh a lot are happier. People who laugh more tend to have higher levels of self-esteem. They also tend to be healthier. Laughter is so important for our general well-being that some people go to "laugh therapy" where they laugh with groups of people.

3. We spend most of our daily lives at work. Our work can increase our happiness. In many countries, a lot of people choose their job based on how much it pays, or on what other people think about that job. But in Denmark, one of the world's happiest countries, most people take jobs that interest them. That gives them a better chance to feel good about the work that they do.

F | Rewrite the two topic sentences that are weak.

1. _____

2. _____

A | Planning. Follow the steps to make notes for your paragraph. Don't write complete sentences. Pay attention to the content more than the grammar or spelling.

Step 1 Look at your brainstorming notes on page 15. Do you think people in your community are generally happy or unhappy? Write a topic sentence for your paragraph in the chart below.

Step 2 Choose the best two or three ideas from your notes and write them in the chart.

Step 3 For each idea, write one or two reasons why it makes people in your community happy or unhappy.

Outline

Topic: Are people in your community generally happy or unhappy?

Topic Sentence	
Brainstorming Idea 1	
Reason(s) this makes you happy / unhappy	
Brainstorming Idea 2	
Reason(s) this makes you happy / unhappy	
Brainstorming Idea 3	
Reason(s) this makes you happy / unhappy	

B | Draft 1. Use your notes to write a first draft of your paragraph.

WRITING TASK: Revising

C | Analyzing. The paragraphs below are on the topic of a happy life.

Which is the first draft? _____   Which is the revision? _____

ⓐ I think I'm generally happy because I like most things about my life. I have a great job. I do work that I feel passionate about, and I like my coworkers. My family and friends are very supportive. Whenever I have problems, I know that my family and friends will help me. Also, my friends make me laugh a lot. In addition, I'm healthy. I don't have any illnesses, and I play fun sports such as soccer and basketball.

ⓑ I think I'm generally happy. I have a great job. I do work that I feel passionate about, and I like my coworkers. I don't make a lot of money, so sometimes I have to do extra work on the weekends. I want to ask for a raise at work. My family and friends are very supportive. Whenever I have problems, I know that my family and friends will help me. Also, my friends make me laugh a lot. In addition, I'm healthy.

D | Analyzing. Work with a partner. Compare the paragraphs above by answering the following questions about each one.

	a		b	
1. Does the paragraph have one main idea?	Y	N	Y	N
2. Does a strong topic sentence introduce the main idea?	Y	N	Y	N
3. Does the paragraph include 2–3 different ideas that relate to the main idea?	Y	N	Y	N
4. Does the paragraph include 1–2 reasons for each one?	Y	N	Y	N
5. Is there any information that doesn't belong?	Y	N	Y	N
6. Is the present tense used correctly?	Y	N	Y	N

Now discuss your answer to this question: Which paragraph is better? Why?

E | Revising. Answer the questions in exercise **D** about your own paragraph.

👥 **F** | **Peer Evaluation.** Exchange your draft with a partner and follow these steps:

Step 1 Read your partner's paragraph and tell him or her one thing that you liked about it.

Step 2 Complete the chart with information from your partner's paragraph.

Topic Sentence _____

Idea 1 _____

Reason(s) this makes
people happy / unhappy _____

_____

Idea 2 _____

Reason(s) this makes
people happy / unhappy _____

_____

Idea 3 _____

Reason(s) this makes
people happy / unhappy _____

_____

Step 3 Compare your chart with the chart your partner completed on page 17.

Step 4 The two charts should be similar. If they aren't, discuss how they differ.

G | **Draft 2.** Write a second draft of your paragraph. Use what you learned from the peer evaluation activity, and your answers to exercise **E**. Make any other necessary changes.

H | **Editing Practice.** Read the information in the box. Then find and correct one simple present tense mistake in each of the sentences (1–5).

> In sentences using the simple present, remember to:
> - use the correct verb endings with third person singular subjects (*he likes, she takes*).
> - watch out for verbs that have irregular forms in the simple present: *be, have,* and *do.*

1. I enjoy the work that I do because it's very challenging, but I doesn't like my boss or my coworkers.

2. My coworkers are supportive, friendly, and fun, and I enjoying spending time with them after work.

3. It's important to me to spend time with my family members when I can, but it's difficult because they don't lives close to me.

4. Although my house is not big and fancy, my neighborhood are safe and beautiful.

5. My friends and I exercises together every day to stay healthy, and that contributes to our happiness.

I | **Editing Checklist.** Use the checklist to find errors in your second draft.

Editing Checklist	Yes	No
1. Are all the words spelled correctly?		
2. Is the first word of every sentence capitalized?		
3. Does every sentence end with the correct punctuation?		
4. Do your subjects and verbs agree?		
5. Did you use the simple present tense correctly?		

J | **Final Draft.** Now use your Editing CheckList to write a third draft of your paragraph. Make any other necessary changes.

UNIT QUIZ

p.2   1. According to the World Database of Happiness, the happiest country in the world is _____.

p.4   2. The level of a person's comfort and wealth is called their _____ of living.

p.5   3. In _____, the government creates jobs and tops up minimum-wage salaries.

p.6   4. In _____, people spend a lot of time socializing, which may contribute to their happiness.

p.8   5. The most important idea of a paragraph is called the _____.

p.12   6. Volunteering can help you forget about your own problems and make you feel _____ for the things you have.

p.13   7. According to researchers, each _____ that we have improves our mood by nine percent.

p.13   8. According to Dan Buettner, your _____ is the most important factor that determines your level of happiness.

Big Ideas

ACADEMIC PATHWAYS

Lesson A: Understanding a biographical text
Identifying supporting ideas
Lesson B: Ranking ideas in order of priority
Lesson C: Supporting the main idea and giving details
Writing a descriptive paragraph

Think and Discuss

1. Do you know any famous inventors?
What did they invent?

2. What inventions are you using right now?

▲ Tiny silica balls, each one 120 nanometers (0.000000012 m) wide, kill cancer cells in a person's body. Nanotechnology was invented in the late twentieth century and is used in many modern inventions.

Exploring the Theme

Read the information on these pages and discuss the questions.

1. Do you agree with the list of the most important inventions? Can you think of other inventions to add?
2. In your opinion, which inventions made the biggest changes to our daily lives? How?
3. Which inventions saved the most lives? How?

What's the World's Greatest Invention?

A U.K. company, Tesco Mobile, asked 4,000 people to name the world's most important invention. Some inventions—like the washing machine and wheel—make everyday life easier. Some, like the medicine penicillin, save lives. Others—like wireless technology and the Internet—changed the way we communicate. As Lance Batchelor, CEO of Tesco Mobile, says, "All of the inventions in this list have changed the world forever."

1 **wheel**

2 **airplane**

3 **lightbulb**

4 **Internet**

5 **personal computer**

6 **telephone**

7 **penicillin**

8 **iPhone**

9 **flushing toilet**

10 **combustion engine**

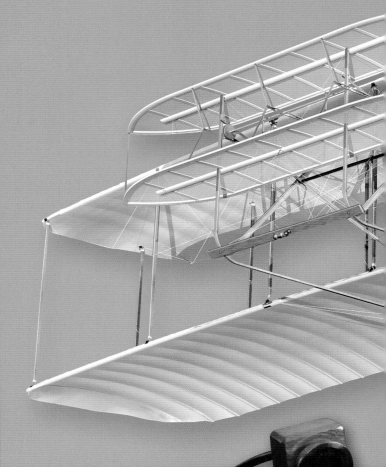

Alexander Graham Bell invented the first **telephone** in 1876. His early interest in speech, sound, and music helped him understand how sound might travel along a wire. Later he created the Bell Telephone Company, which became AT&T, the largest phone company in the U.S.

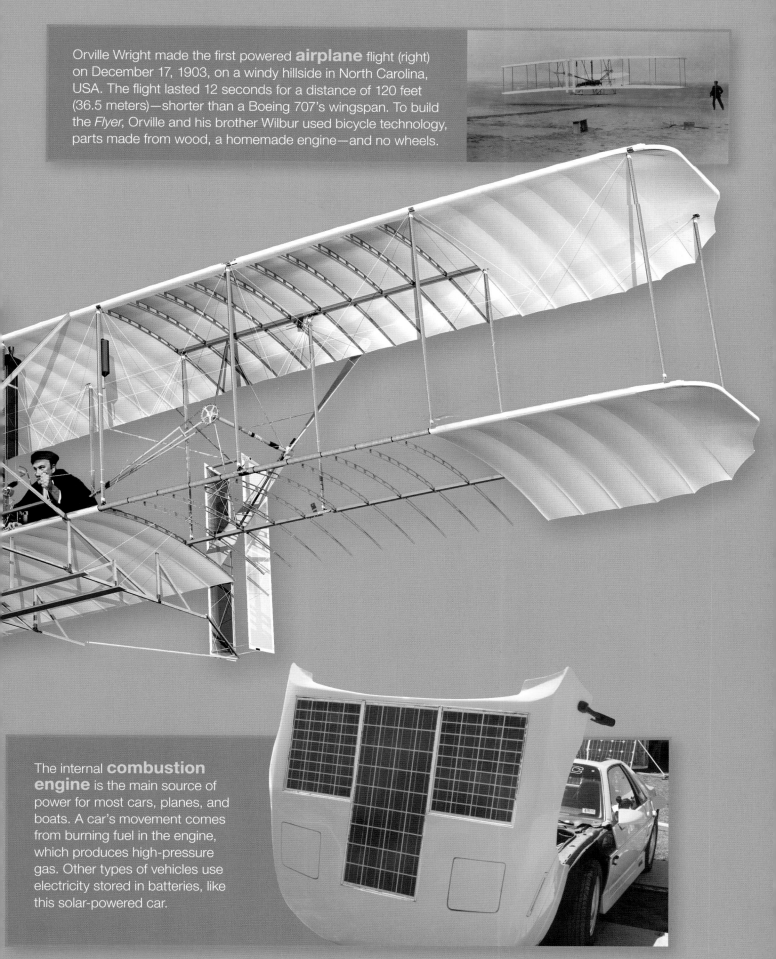

Orville Wright made the first powered **airplane** flight (right) on December 17, 1903, on a windy hillside in North Carolina, USA. The flight lasted 12 seconds for a distance of 120 feet (36.5 meters)—shorter than a Boeing 707's wingspan. To build the *Flyer*, Orville and his brother Wilbur used bicycle technology, parts made from wood, a homemade engine—and no wheels.

The internal **combustion engine** is the main source of power for most cars, planes, and boats. A car's movement comes from burning fuel in the engine, which produces high-pressure gas. Other types of vehicles use electricity stored in batteries, like this solar-powered car.

A | **Building Vocabulary.** Find the words in **blue** in the reading passage on pages 25–26. Read the words around them and try to guess their meanings. Then write each word next to its definition.

1. _____ (verb) have enough money to pay for something

2. _____ (verb) gave the energy that something needed in order to work

3. _____ (adjective) able to do tasks well without wasting time or energy

4. _____ (noun) a form of energy that can be used for heating and lighting and to provide energy for machines

5. _____ (noun) energy from the sun's light and heat

6. _____ (adjective) having the ability to invent and develop new and original ideas

7. _____ (adverb) in the end, especially after a lot of problems

8. _____ (noun) the act of making sure that something does not happen

9. _____ (noun) the things people need for a job, hobby, or sport

10. _____ (noun) a drawing that shows how to make something

B | **Using Vocabulary.** Answer the questions. Share your ideas with a partner.

1. Describe one way in which you are **creative**.

2. What **equipment** do you use for your job or for your hobby?

3. **Solar power** is one source of energy. What are some other ways to produce **electricity**?

C | **Brainstorming.** Make a list of things you use every day that require electricity.

1. _____   5. _____
2. _____   6. _____
3. _____   7. _____
4. _____   8. _____

D | **Predicting.** Read the title and look at the photos on pages 25–26. What do you think the reading is about? Write one sentence.

A Man who invention the wind will for save his country.

> **Word Link**
>
> The suffix **-tion** can turn some verbs into nouns,
> e.g., prevent / prevention, define / definition, act / action, create / creation, contribute / contribution.

Malawi

The Power of Creativity

track 1-04

A
WILLIAM KAMKWAMBA lives in Malawi, Africa, where most people have to grow their own food and have no electricity or running water.[1] Only two percent of Malawians can afford electricity. With no electricity or running water, life is difficult. In 2001, when William was 14 years old, life in Malawi became even more difficult. There was a severe drought[2] and most families, including William's, couldn't grow enough food. He explains, "Within five months all Malawians began to starve to death. My family ate one meal per day, at night."

B
Because of the drought, William's family couldn't afford to send him to school anymore. So one day William went to the library near his home. He wanted to continue his education. William found a science book called *Using Energy*. It included instructions for building a windmill. Windmills can be very efficient sources of electricity, and they can bring water up from underground. William didn't know much English, and he wasn't able to understand most of the book, but it was full of pictures and diagrams.[3] Looking at the pictures, William thought he could build a windmill for his family.

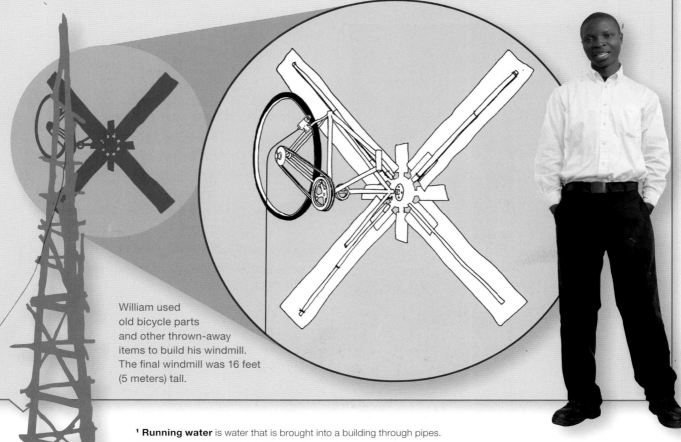

William used old bicycle parts and other thrown-away items to build his windmill. The final windmill was 16 feet (5 meters) tall.

[1] **Running water** is water that is brought into a building through pipes.
[2] A **drought** is a long period of time with no rain.
[3] **Diagrams** are drawings that show how something, e.g., a machine, works.

When William went home and started building his windmill, a lot of people laughed at him, including his mother. They didn't think he could do it, but William was confident. He saw the photo of the windmill in the book. That meant someone else was able to build it, so he knew he could build it, too. William was also creative. He didn't have the parts and equipment that he saw in the book's illustrations, and he couldn't buy them. So he looked for parts in junkyards.[4] He explains, "I found a tractor fan,[5] [a] shock absorber,[6] [and] PVC pipes.[7] Using a bicycle frame . . . , I built my machine."

William changed and improved his design little by little. First, the windmill powered only one lightbulb. Eventually, it powered four lights. Then there was enough electricity for four lights and a radio. No one laughed at William after that, and people in his town started to come to his house to get power for their cell

phones. Later, William built a second windmill. This one brought water up from underground. After that, William began to teach other people how to build windmills. He also continued to build more of them himself, including one at a primary school in Malawi.

Because of his success with the windmills, William was able to go back to school. He also helped with other projects, including solar power, clean water, and malaria[8] prevention. He wrote a book about his life, *The Boy Who Harnessed the Wind: Creating Currents of Electricity and Hope.* In addition, he uses his website, movingwindmills.org, to educate and give hope to people. His main message is this: "To the Africans, and the poor who are struggling[9] with your dreams . . . trust yourself and believe. Whatever happens, don't give up."[10]

---

[4] A **junkyard** is a place where old machines are thrown away.

[5] A **tractor fan** is a machine part that helps cool the engine in a tractor (a vehicle used on farms).

[6] A **shock absorber** is a machine part that helps make a car run smoothly over uneven roads.

[7] **PVC pipes** are tubes made from a plastic material (polyvinyl chloride).

[8] **Malaria** is a disease spread by mosquitoes.

[9] If someone is **struggling**, they are trying hard to do something because it is difficult.

[10] If you **don't give up**, you don't stop trying to do something, especially something that is difficult.

A | **Understanding the Gist.** What is the main idea of the reading? Circle the best answer. Then compare with your prediction on page 24.

1. Windmills can create electricity and bring up water from under the ground.
2. In most parts of Malawi, there is no electricity or running water.
3. A young boy used his creativity to bring electricity to his village.

B | **Identifying Key Details.** Complete the sentences below with information from the reading.

1. In 2001, life became very challenging for William's family because _a drought_.
2. William found instructions for a windmill in a book called _Using energy_.
3. When he started to build his windmill, many people in his village _laughed at him_.
4. He knew that he could build the windmill because _his creative_.
5. After William built his first windmill, people came to his house to _charged their phones._.
6. William's second windmill was able to _bring water up from the underground_.

C | **Critical Thinking: Making Connections.** Complete the chart below. Fill in the missing problems and solutions.

Problems				
William couldn't afford to go to school.	William couldn't read the book about windmills because he didn't know much English.	he don't have equipment.	The village needed more water.	Other people wanted to build windmills but didn't know how.

Solutions				
he went to liberty.	he look at picture.	William went to a junkyard.	he built the second windmill for bring water.	he taught them.

D | **Personalizing.** Write answers to the questions.

1. Name a problem that you solved in your own life. How did you solve the problem? _____

2. Choose one of the inventions from page 22 or use your own idea. Describe the problem(s) that it solved.

   Invention: _____

   Problem(s) it solved: _____

Reading Skill: *Identifying Supporting Ideas*

Supporting ideas tell more about the main idea. They can do the following:

describe   give reasons   give examples

Look at the paragraph from the reading. What does each colored sentence do?

When William went home and started building his windmill, a lot of people laughed at him, including his mother. They didn't think he could do it, but William was confident. He saw the photo of the windmill in the book. That meant someone else was able to build it, so he knew he could build it, too. William was also creative. He didn't have the parts and equipment that he saw in the book's illustrations, and he couldn't buy them. So he looked for parts in junkyards. He explains, "I found a tractor fan, shock absorber, [and] PVC pipes. Using a bicycle frame ... , I built my machine."

The main idea of the paragraph is that William was confident and creative in building his windmill. The green sentences **give reasons** why William was confident. The blue sentences **give examples** of how William was creative. And the purple sentences **describe** how he did it.

A | **Analyzing.** Read the information about seat belts below. Write the main idea of the paragraph and the three supporting details

Main idea: _____

Supporting detail 1: _____

Supporting detail 2: _____

Supporting detail 3: _____

track **1-05**

Many inventions change lives, but Nils Bohlin's invention has probably helped to save more than a million lives so far. Bohlin invented a new type of seat belt that is in all cars made today. Before Bohlin's invention, seat belts were buckled across the stomach (see picture). The buckles often caused injuries during high-speed accidents. Bohlin's seat belt holds the upper and lower body safely in place, with a buckle at the side.

buckle ▶

B | **Identifying Supporting Details.** Look back at the reading passage on pages 25–26. Find and underline one supporting detail that gives a reason, one that gives an example, and one that describes.

Solar Cooking

Before Viewing

A | **Matching.** Here are some words you will hear in the video. Write each word or phrase next to the correct definition. Use your dictionary to help you.

absorb	alternative
developing world	fuel
pollution	purify

1. _____ the process of making things such as air and water dirty

2. _____ to take in something, such as gas, liquid, or heat

3. _____ countries or parts of the world that generally have low standards of living

4. _____ to make something clean by removing harmful or dangerous things from it

5. _____ a different choice

6. _____ things that provide heat or energy, such as oil, wood, or gasoline

B | **Brainstorming.** Many people in developing countries have to burn wood to cook their food. Why do you think this might be a problem?

can cause air pollution _____ _____

While Viewing

A | Watch the video about solar cooking. Does it mention any of the things that you listed in exercise **B** above? Circle any items that are mentioned.

B | As you view the video, think about the answers to these questions.

1. How do solar stoves work?

2. What can a person do with a solar stove? Who can benefit from them?

3. How much does a solar stove cost and how long can it last?

▲ Cooking in many African countries is done the traditional way, over a wood fire.

After Viewing

A | Discuss answers to questions 1–3 above with a partner.

B | **Critical Thinking: Synthesizing.** In what ways are William Kamkwamba's windmills and the solar cooker in the video similar?

_____

_____

A | Building Vocabulary. Read the sentences below. Use the context to help you identify the part of speech (adjective, noun, verb) and meaning of each **bold** word. Write your answers. Check your answers in a dictionary.

1. Bottles are useful **containers** for water and other liquids. They make liquids easy to carry.

   Part of speech: _____

   Meaning: _____

2. Doctors have many different ways to **detect** diseases. For example, they can do blood tests or listen to your lungs to learn if you are sick.

   Part of speech: _____

   Meaning: _____

3. Solar power can **benefit** people in the developing world by providing them with free electricity.

   Part of speech: _____

   Meaning: _____

4. Cell phones can make a noise to **indicate** that you are receiving a text message.

   Part of speech: _____

   Meaning: _____

5. There have already been several **innovations** in this century. Text messaging and the tablet computer are just two examples.

   Part of speech: _____

   Meaning: _____

6. The cell phone is a popular **device** for things such as communication and Internet browsing. For things such as document creation and movie watching, a computer is a better choice.

   Part of speech: _____

   Meaning: _____

Word Link

The suffix
-able can turn
some verbs
into adjectives,
e.g., renew /
renew**able**, detect
/ detect**able**,
afford / afford**able**,
prevent /
prevent**able**.

7. The sun is a great source of **renewable** energy because we can't use up all the sun's heat and light.

   Part of speech: _____

   Meaning: _____

8. Before refrigerators were invented, people could not **store** fresh meat. Instead, they had to store salted or dried meat.

Part of speech: _____

Meaning: _____

9. Morse code was invented in the 1930s. It is a **system** of communication that uses long and short sounds.

Part of speech: _____

Meaning: _____

10. The wheel is one of the most **valuable** inventions of all time. Without it, we would probably have to walk or ride on the backs of animals to travel long distances.

Part of speech: _____

Meaning: _____

B | Using Vocabulary. Answer the questions in complete sentences. Then share your sentences with a partner.

1. What do you think is the most **valuable innovation** of the last 10 years? Why?

_____

2. What are some examples of **renewable** energy?

_____

3. What **devices** do you use every day?

_____

4. What kinds of things **indicate** a person's mood?

_____

5. What **system** do you use for remembering your schedule?

_____

C | Predicting. Look at the photos, and read the title, subheads, and opening paragraph of the reading passage on pages 32–33. What do you think is the purpose of each of the items described? Discuss your ideas with a partner.

Infant Warmer _____

Water Container _____

Portable Clay Cooler _____

Health Detector _____

Solar Wi-Fi Light _____

Strategy

Use clues in titles, headings, pictures, and captions to get a quick sense of what you will read. As you read in more detail, check whether your predictions were correct.

Big Ideas: Little Packages

track 1-06

CAN SIMPLE IDEAS change the world? They just might, one new idea at a time. Creative designers and scientists are working to invent products for communities in developing countries. Some of their innovations might solve even the biggest problems—from health care to clean water.

▲ Developers of the Embrace Infant Warmer (left to right): Naganand Murty, Linus Liang, Rahul Panicker, Jane Chen.

Infant Warmer

Around 19 million low-birthweight babies are born every year in developing countries. These babies weigh less than 5.5 pounds (2.5 kilograms) when they're born. Low-birthweight babies are often unable to keep their body temperatures[1] warm enough. Many get too cold and die. The Embrace Infant Warmer helps keep these babies warm. Developer Jane Chen says, "Over the next five years, we hope to save the lives of almost a million babies."

◄ "We hope that the Embrace Infant Warmer represents a new trend for the future of technology," says developer Jane Chen. "Simple, localized, affordable solutions that have the potential to make a huge social impact."

Water Container

In poor areas, people often have to walk several miles to get clean water. Usually, women and children have to carry heavy containers of water home every day, and it is difficult work. The Q Drum holds 13 gallons (about 50 liters) in a rolling container. With this innovation, people can easily roll the water on the ground.

[1] Your **body temperature** is how hot or how cold your body is.

Portable Clay Cooler

D The pot-in-pot system is a good way to store food without using electricity. The user puts wet sand between two pots, one fitting inside the other. The water evaporates[2] and keeps food cool. That helps food stay fresh longer. For example, tomatoes can last weeks instead of just days. That way, people can buy more fresh fruits and vegetables at the market, and farmers can make more money.

Health Detector

E Scientist Hayat Sindi's device is the size of a postage stamp, and it costs just a penny. But it could save millions of lives. In many parts of the world, doctors and nurses work with no electricity or clean water. They have to send health tests to labs[3] and wait weeks for results. But this little piece of paper could change that. It contains tiny holes that are filled with chemicals. These chemicals can detect health problems. A person places a single drop of blood on the paper. The chemicals in the paper change because of the blood and indicate whether or not the person has an illness.

▲ Saudi-born inventor, Hayat Sindi, presenting her invention at the 2009 Pop!Tech conference.

Solar Wi-Fi Light

F The StarSight system is an innovation that can benefit millions of people around the world. It absorbs solar energy during the day to power streetlamps at night. The solar panels also power wireless Internet access. The result: renewable electricity for better street lighting and faster communication. This can be extremely valuable in places where it is difficult to get electricity.

[2] When a liquid **evaporates**, it changes to a gas as its temperature increases.
[3] **Labs** are laboratories, places where scientific research is done.

A | **Understanding the Gist.** Look back at your answers for exercise **C** on page 31. Were your predictions correct?

B | **Identifying Key Details.** Read the following sentences about the reading on pages 32–33. For each sentence, circle **T** (true), **F** (false), or **NG** (the information is not given in the passage).

1. The infant warmer was invented to help low-birthweight babies.   **T**   F   NG

2. In poor areas, men and teenage boys usually carry water home.   T   **F**   NG

3. The portable clay cooler will cause farmers to make less money because people won't have to buy vegetables every day.   T   **F**   NG

4. Hayat Sindi's low-tech diagnostic device is made of paper.   **T**   F   NG

5. Each solar Wi-Fi light can provide electricity for 10 to 20 homes at a time.   T   F   **NG**

C | **Identifying Supporting Ideas.** Find supporting details in the reading to answer each question below.

1. What is the reason that low-birthweight babies need infant warmers?

It help to keep the low - birthweight babies warm

2. What can the Q Drum hold?

13 gallons of water.

3. How does the portable clay cooler work?

put wet sand between two pots, one lifting inside the other water will keep cool.

4. What is one reason that people need Hayat Sindi's diagnostic tool?

It's cheap.

5. What is an example of how the solar Wi-Fi light can benefit people?

It can keep the solar energy and use at night.

CT Focus

To rank items in order, first decide on your *criteria* for ranking, e.g., how many people you think will be able to afford the item, or how many lives might be saved or improved.

D | **Critical Thinking: Ranking and Justifying.** Which of the innovations from pages 32–33 do you think is the most important? Which is the least important? Rank them 1–5, with 1 as the most important. Then talk with a partner and explain your choices.

_1_ Infant Warmer   _3_ Portable Clay Cooler   _4_ Solar Wi-Fi Light

_2_ Water Container   _5_ Health Detector

E | **Critical Thinking: Synthesizing.** Discuss this question in small groups: How is the clay cooler described in the reading similar to, and different from, the solar cooker shown in the video?

GOAL: In this lesson, you are going to plan, write, revise, and edit a paragraph. Your topic is:
Choose an innovation—one from this unit or one you have used yourself.
Describe the need it filled and how it changed people's lives.

A | Read the information in the box. Then use the simple past tense of the verbs in parentheses to complete the sentences (1–7).

Language for Writing: Review of the Simple Past

We use the simple past tense to talk about events that began and ended in the past.

> *According to historians, a man named Ts'ai Lun **invented** paper in China around AD 105.*
>
> *Before that time, people **didn't have** inexpensive material to write on.*
>
> *People **wrote** on things such as silk and clay, which **were** expensive and inconvenient.*

To form the simple past tense of *be*:
- use *was* or *were* to form affirmative statements.
- use *was not / wasn't* or *were not / weren't* to form negative statements.

To form the simple past tense with other verbs:
- add *-ed* to the end of most verbs to form affirmative statements.
- use *did not / didn't* with the base form of a main verb to form negative statements.

Some verbs have irregular past tense forms in affirmative statements:
go—went   have—had   make—made   take—took   do—did   build—built

For more explanation and examples, see page 215.

Example: In 2001, there ___was___ (be) a drought in Malawi and most people
___didn't have___ (not / have) enough food.

1. Most people in William Kamkwamba's village ___didn't have___ (not / have) electricity.

2. William ___went___ (go) to the library.

3. He ___found___ (find) a book there called *Using Energy.*

4. William ___used___ (use) the information in the book and he ___built___ (build) a windmill.

5. When he ___started___ (start), people ___didn't believe___ (not / believe) that he could do it.

6. William ___wasn't___ (not / be) worried. He ___was___ (be) confident.

7. After a while, he ___was___ (be) successful. His windmill ___made___ (make) electricity.

B | **Applying.** Write five sentences using the simple past tense. Describe things that people did not do 50 years ago, but that you do today.

C | **Brainstorming.** Brainstorm a list of innovations that you think are important. Use ideas from this unit or your own ideas.

_____

_____

D | **Journal Writing.** Use your ideas from exercise **C** to write a response in your journal to the following question. Write for three minutes.

Which innovations caused the biggest changes in people's lives?

Writing Skill: _Supporting the Main Idea and Giving Details_

Good paragraphs include supporting ideas that give information and details about the main idea. These sentences can give descriptions, reasons, or examples to help the reader clearly understand the main idea.

E | **Identifying Supporting Ideas.** Match each topic sentence with three supporting sentences. Write **A** or **B** for each one. Two sentences are extra.

Topic Sentence A: About 900 million people need access to safe drinking water, and a simple invention may be the answer to this problem.

Topic Sentence B: The solar-powered MightyLight is a safe and clean source of lighting that can provide light to millions of people around the world.

_A_ a. The LifeStraw provides instant clean water, saving lives during disasters.

_A_ b. You should drink about eight glasses of water a day.

_B_ c. The MightyLight is safer and cleaner than traditional kerosene lamps.

_A_ d. Each straw purifies about 160 gallons of water.

_B_ e. It's easy to carry, and you can hang it on a wall or place it on a tabletop.

_B_ f. Candles don't provide much light.

_B_ g. It also lasts longer—its LED technology is good for up to 30 years.

_A_ h. Thousands of LifeStraws were donated to Haiti after the 2010 earthquake.

F | Now use the sentences in exercise **E** to write two paragraphs.

A | Planning. Follow the steps to make notes for your paragraph. Don't write complete sentences. Pay attention to the content more than the grammar or spelling.

Step 1: From your brainstorming notes on page 36, choose an innovation to write about.

Step 2: Write a topic sentence that will introduce your paragraph.

Step 3: Look at your brainstorming notes again. Complete the chart.

Outline

Topic: Choose an invention. What need did it fill, and how did it change people's lives?

Topic Sentence	Cell phone is important for human life
Supporting Idea What is one way that the innovation changed people's lives?	We use in daily life and its can make every easy.
Detail(s) (one or two points)	Cell phone is real important because you can connect with another people and can use internet to get some information you want.
Supporting Idea What is another way that the innovation changed people's lives?	We can use for investigate and got knowledge from something.
Detail(s) (one or two points)	If you want to know about some fact, it's very easy to read from some research. you could find them on the internet system.

B | Draft 1. Use your notes to write a first draft of your paragraph.

C | **Analyzing.** The paragraphs below are on the topic of an innovation.

Which is the first draft? _____   Which is the revision? _____

ⓐ   The car is one of the most important inventions in history. Before the car was invented, most people used horses to travel long distances, and they didn't travel very quickly. For example, a person on a horse could travel an average of 50–60 miles in a day. People traveling by horse and carriage could go 20–30 miles in a day. Because it was difficult to travel far, most people stayed in their own towns and villages their whole lives. Families stayed in the same place for generations. Now that we have cars, it only takes an hour to go 60 miles. Because it's so easy to travel long distances, people can work 60 miles away from home if they want to. And they can live almost anywhere they want. Because of the car, people have many more opportunities to shape their lives than they used to.

ⓑ   The car is one of the most important inventions in history. The first real car factory opened in 1902. Before the car was invented, most people used horses to travel long distances, and they didn't travel very quickly. For example, a person on a horse could travel an average of 50–60 miles in a day. People traveling by horse and carriage could go 20–30 miles in a day. A horse can go up to 40 miles per hour, but it gets tired after just a few miles. If the horse goes more slowly, it can travel for a longer period of time without getting tired. Now that we have cars, it only takes an hour to go 60 miles. Because it's so easy to travel long distances, people can work 60 miles away from home if they want to. And they can live almost anywhere they want. Because of the car, people have many more opportunities to shape their lives than they used to.

D | **Analyzing.** Work with a partner. Compare the paragraphs above by answering the following questions about each one.

	ⓐ	ⓑ
1. Does the paragraph have one main idea?	Y N	Y N
2. Does the topic sentence introduce the main idea?	Y N	Y N
3. Does the paragraph include 2–3 supporting ideas?	Y N	Y N
4. Does the paragraph include 1–2 details for each supporting idea?	Y N	Y N
5. Is there any information that doesn't belong?	Y N	Y N
6. Does the paragraph use the past tense correctly?	Y N	Y N

E | **Revising.** Answer the questions in exercise **D** about your own paragraph.

F | **Peer Evaluation.** Exchange your draft with a partner and follow these steps:

Step 1   Read your partner's paragraph and tell him or her one thing that you liked about it.

Step 2   Complete the chart below with information from your partner's paragraph.

Topic Sentence	_____
Supporting Idea What is one way that the innovation changed people's lives?	_____ _____ _____
Detail(s) (*one or two points*)	_____ _____
Supporting Idea What is another way that the innovation changed people's lives?	_____ _____
Detail(s) (*one or two points*)	_____ _____

Step 3   Compare your chart with the chart your partner completed on page 37.

Step 4   The two charts should be similar. If they aren't, discuss how they differ.

G | **Draft 2.** Write a second draft of your paragraph. Use what you learned from the peer evaluation activity, and your answers to exercise **E**. Make any other necessary changes.

H | **Editing Practice.** Read the information in the box. Then find and correct one simple past tense mistake in each of the sentences (1–5).

> In sentences using the **simple past tense**, remember to:
> - use the correct past tense forms of *be*: *was*, *wasn't*, *were*, and *weren't*.
> - use the correct verb endings; for most verbs, you add *-ed* to form the simple past tense, but some verbs have irregular past tense forms.
> - use the base form of the verb with *did not / didn't* in negative statements.

1. The people in William Kamkwamba's village wasn't confident about William's plan.
2. When they were young, the Wright brothers haved a flying toy.
3. Alexander Graham Bell make the first telephone.
4. The first car didn't went very fast.
5. Ts'ai Lun invented paper in the first century AD, but paper didn't be widely available until many years later.

WRITING TASK: Editing

I | Editing Checklist. Use the checklist to find errors in your second draft.

Editing Checklist	Yes	No
1. Are all the words spelled correctly?		
2. Is the first word of every sentence capitalized?		
3. Does every sentence end with the correct punctuation?		
4. Do your subjects and verbs agree?		
5. Did you use the simple present and simple past correctly?		

J | Final Draft. Now use your Editing Checklist to write a third draft of your paragraph. Make any other necessary changes.

UNIT QUIZ

p.22　　1. According to a U.K. survey, the wheel is the world's most _____.

p.24　　2. Energy from the sun is called _____ power.

p.25　　3. Windmills can create _____ and bring up _____ from under the ground.

p.28　　4. Supporting sentences can _____, _____, and _____.

p.29　　5. A(n) _____ uses power from the sun to heat food for eating. It is also called a(n) _____.

p.30　　6. A new thing or method of doing something is called a(n) _____.

p.33　　7. Hayat Sindi's health detector is as small as a(n) _____.

p.39　　8. We use the _____ of a verb with *did not / didn't* to make a past tense negative statement.

Connected Lives

Think and Discuss

1. How do you use the Internet to keep in touch with other people?
2. In what ways is the Internet useful for teaching and learning?

▲ Internet users gather at a Wi-Fi cafe on 42nd Street, New York.

Exploring the Theme

A. Look at the information below and answer the questions.

1. What do the colors on the map show?
2. Which places are most connected? Which regions had the biggest rise in Internet use?

B. Look at the information on page 43 and answer the questions.

1. What information does the graphic show? Do you think the connections are different today?
2. Which social networks are popular in your country today? Why are they popular?

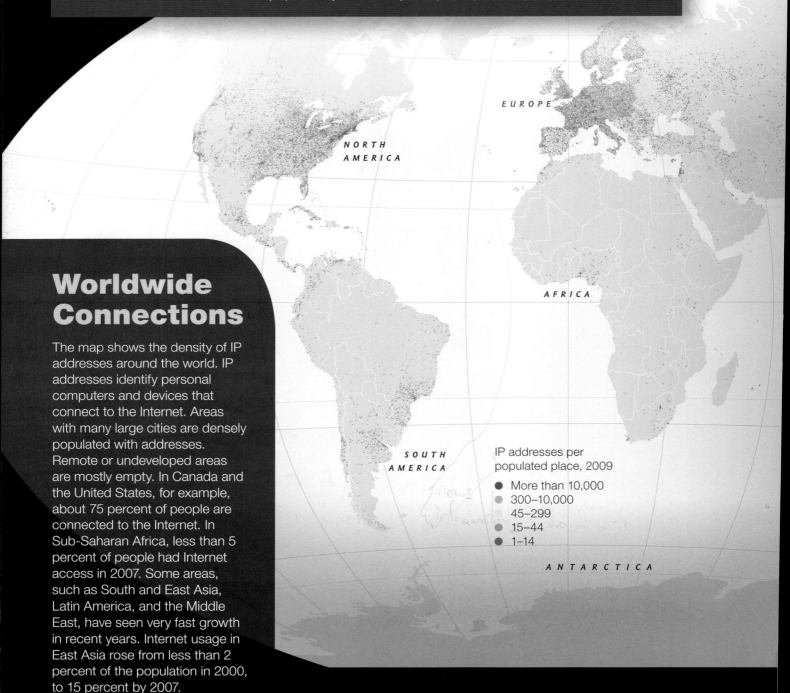

Worldwide Connections

The map shows the density of IP addresses around the world. IP addresses identify personal computers and devices that connect to the Internet. Areas with many large cities are densely populated with addresses. Remote or undeveloped areas are mostly empty. In Canada and the United States, for example, about 75 percent of people are connected to the Internet. In Sub-Saharan Africa, less than 5 percent of people had Internet access in 2007. Some areas, such as South and East Asia, Latin America, and the Middle East, have seen very fast growth in recent years. Internet usage in East Asia rose from less than 2 percent of the population in 2000, to 15 percent by 2007.

NORTH AMERICA

EUROPE

AFRICA

SOUTH AMERICA

ANTARCTICA

IP addresses per populated place, 2009

- More than 10,000
- 300–10,000
- 45–299
- 15–44
- 1–14

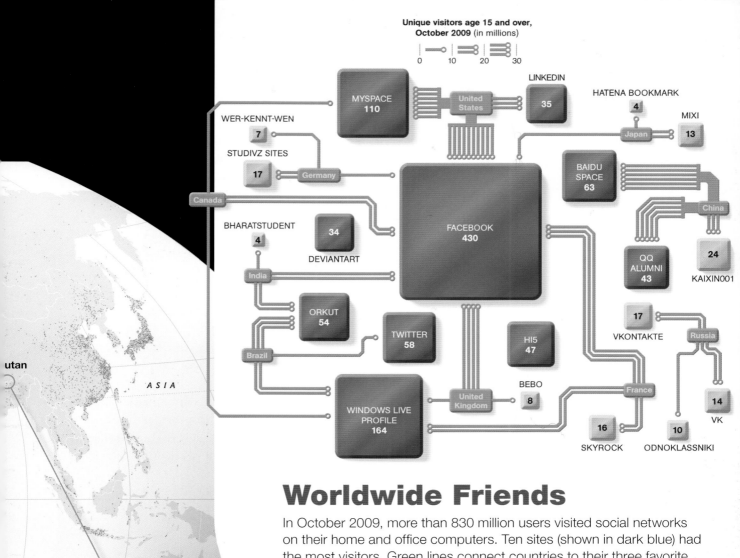

Unique visitors age 15 and over, October 2009 (in millions)

0   10   20   30

LINKEDIN
35

HATENA BOOKMARK
4

MYSPACE
110

United States

MIXI
13

WER-KENNT-WEN
7

Japan

STUDIVZ SITES
17

Germany

BAIDU SPACE
63

Canada

China

BHARATSTUDENT
4

DEVIANTART
34

FACEBOOK
430

QQ ALUMNI
43

KAIXIN001
24

India

ORKUT
54

TWITTER
58

HI5
47

VKONTAKTE
17

Russia

Brazil

VK
14

United Kingdom

BEBO
8

France

WINDOWS LIVE PROFILE
164

SKYROCK
16

ODNOKLASSNIKI
10

Worldwide Friends

In October 2009, more than 830 million users visited social networks on their home and office computers. Ten sites (shown in dark blue) had the most visitors. Green lines connect countries to their three favorite sites. The number of social network users continues to grow: By 2012, Facebook alone had more than 800 million active users.

The remote kingdom of Bhutan ▶ introduced its first Internet service in 1999. The country's first Internet café opened a year later. Today, the Internet helps young Bhutanese, such as these college students, stay connected with the rest of the world.

A | **Building Vocabulary.** Find the words in **blue** in the reading passage on pages 45–46. Read the words around them and try to guess their meanings. Then match the sentence parts below to make definitions.

1. ___d___ When you **edit** something,
2. ___a___ A **culture** is a society with
3. ___e___ **Communication** means
4. ___b___ When you **interact** with someone,
5. ___g___ The **relationship** between two people is
6. ___i___ The term **media** includes
7. ___f___ **Participation** means
8. ___c___ Something with **potential** has
9. ___j___ **Technology** is
10. ___h___ If something is **traditional**,

a. its own beliefs or way of life.
b. you talk, spend time, or work together.
c. the possibility for success in the future.
d. you correct and make changes to it in order to improve it.
e. sharing information with people, for example, by talking or writing.
f. joining in to be a part of something.
g. the way they feel and act toward each other, or the way they are connected.
h. it is connected with customs, methods, or beliefs that have existed for a long time.
i. television, radio, magazines, and other things that provide information.
j. methods, systems, and devices that are the result of scientific knowledge.

B | **Using Vocabulary.** Answer the questions. Share your ideas with a partner.

1. Why do you think classroom **participation** is important for students?
2. What are some of the latest developments in **technology**?
3. What forms of **media** do you use regularly? What do you use them for?

C | **Brainstorming.** Think about how we get and share information by TV and the Internet. How are TV and the Internet similar? How are they different? Write your ideas in the chart.

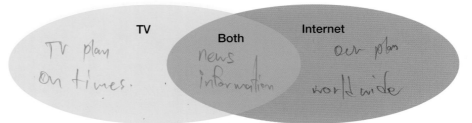

TV — TV play on times.

Both — news information

Internet — Over plan world wide

D | **Predicting.** Scan the reading passage on pages 45–46 quickly. List two other nouns or verbs that appear two or more times.

___relationships___   _____   _____

Now look at the words you wrote. What do you think the passage is about?

a. how the Internet is changing society
b. how to use the Internet in the classroom
c. why websites are the most important form of media

The Changing Face of Communication

▲ Students explore the online world at an Internet café in Novosibirsk, Russia.

A Michael Wesch is a cultural anthropology[1] professor who explores the effects of new media on society and culture. He believes that all human relationships depend on communication. Change the type of communication, and you change the relationships. Change the relationships, and you change the structure[2] of society.

B One example of this, he says, is television. When television became the dominant medium[3] in the 1950s, it changed the way families interacted. Family members began to sit in front of the TV to watch rather than face each other to talk. The people on the television spoke, and the TV viewers listened. In this one-way type of communication, only the people on TV had power. Only they had a voice.[4]

Communication Today: The Internet

C Today, the Internet is changing our relationships again. The newest media of communication are on the Internet, and these media change and grow every day. Wesch and his students study social networks and other interactive Internet sites. For example, they studied YouTube, the popular online video sharing site. As Wesch explains, "Instead of simply watching TV, we can create and edit our own videos." Viewers all over the world can watch and write comments. This kind of sharing changes the way we communicate. With the Internet, everyone can have a voice.

[1] **Anthropology** is the study of people, society, and culture.
[2] The **structure** of something is the way it is put together or organized.
[3] A **dominant medium** is the most powerful, successful, or noticeable medium (*medium* is the singular form of *media*).
[4] A person's **voice** can refer to his or her opinion about something and the ability to share that opinion.

Wesch created and posted his own short video on YouTube. It has had more than 11 million views. The video asks us to think about how we use and interact with the Internet. The Internet is no longer just connecting people with information. It's connecting people with people. It's a way for us to share our thoughts and ideas with the world. It wouldn't exist without us. In fact, Wesch says, "the Web is us."

▲ A computer brings information and entertainment to a class of young Nigerian students.

Education and the New Media

Wesch wants to make changes in education to fit this new style of communication. He has made some changes in his own classes. For example, in his Introduction to Cultural Anthropology class, he didn't simply teach his students about different cultures. Instead, he asked each student to become an expert in one culture. Then the class used their knowledge to create an online role-playing game. As they learned about the different cultures, they increased their knowledge about global problems.

According to Wesch, activities such as the role-play exercise help prepare students to be active and responsible members of society. "I ask [students] to think not about what new media was designed for," he says, "but how they can [use] it for something else." A great example, he believes, is social media. It was created to help friends connect, but now it also allows people to share and collaborate[5] on projects.

Wesch understands that the new media can provide opportunities for sharing and participation. However, he warns that online content can also be misleading. He believes it is important for everyone, especially students, to understand the dangers of digital media and learn how to use it wisely. In a traditional classroom, for example, the teacher is the main provider of information. Now, information is available to anyone with an Internet connection—and anyone can provide new information at any time. So one of the goals of education should be to prepare students to find, analyze, and think critically about online information, as well as create their own.

Wesch says, "I want to believe that technology can help us see relationships and global connections in positive new ways. It's pretty amazing that I have this little box sitting on my desk through which I can talk to any one of a billion people. And yet do any of us really use it for all the potential that's there?"

"One of the most important skills we must now learn is collaboration. We can learn to listen to one another, use each other's strengths, and practice working together in any environment."

- Michael Wesch, U.S. Professor of the Year, 2008

[5] If you **collaborate**, you work with other people to achieve a goal or complete a project.

A | Understanding the Gist. Look back at your answer for exercise **D** on page 44. Was your prediction correct?

B | Identifying Key Details. Complete each statement with information from the reading passage.

1. Some examples of new media are _____ Internet _____.
2. In the 1950s, TV changed _____ families comunication _____.
3. The main way that TV is different from the Internet is _____.
4. One way the Internet can benefit us is _____.
5. One way that the Internet can be harmful is _____.
6. Wesch's students shared cultural information by playing _____ online role play games. _____.
7. Wesch thinks students need to learn how to _____ create their own. _____.

C | Critical Thinking: Making Inferences. Work with a partner. What can you infer from each statement from the reading passage? Circle the best inference.

1. "When television became the dominant medium in the 1950s, it changed the way families interacted."

   (a.) Before the 1950s, a different medium was probably dominant.

   b. There were a lot of good television programs in the 1950s.

2. "This kind of sharing changes the way we communicate. With the Internet, everyone can have a voice."

   (a.) People probably should not share certain things on the Internet.

   b. The Internet is a better medium of communication than TV.

3. "It's pretty amazing that I have this little box sitting on my desk through which I can talk to any one of a billion people. And yet do any of us really use it for all the potential that's there?"

   (a.) There are a lot of possible uses of the Internet that most people don't really think about.

   b. The Internet is an amazing tool, but most people in the world don't use it very much.

> **CT Focus**
>
> You **make inferences** when you make logical guesses about things a writer does not say directly. This is also called "reading between the lines."

D | Personalizing. Write answers to the questions.

1. Do you ever create Web content, write comments on websites, or post things on social networking sites? Why, or why not?

   Yes, because the social networking was opened to write our opinion on it.

2. Do you agree with Wesch's views on how we use the Internet? Why, or why not?

   I agree with him because when you use internet for education, it easy for you to find the information.

Reading Skill: *Skimming for Gist*

Skimming is quickly looking over a passage to get the general idea of what it is about. When we skim, we don't read every word. Instead, we look for important words or chunks (pieces) of information. For example, we look for things such as names, dates, and repeated words.

We often skim online news sites to find out the most important news of the day, blogs to choose which posts we want to read, and magazines to decide what we want to read about. But skimming can also help with academic reading. If you skim a passage before you read it carefully, you can get an idea of what the passage is about and how it is organized. This can help you understand the passage more easily when you do read it carefully, because you know what to expect.

A | Skimming. Skim the paragraph below. Read only the darker words. What do you think is the main idea of the paragraph?

For many of us, visiting Facebook, Twitter, or other online social networks has become a regular part of our daily activities. However, we may not have noticed the significant ways that social networks have changed our lives. First of all, they have changed the way we get our news. These days, we often only read the news stories that our friends post online. Second, our relationships have changed. Now, it's easier to keep in touch with new friends and find old friends that we haven't seen for a long time. Third, many of us share thoughts with our online friends that we used to keep private. For example, in an instant, we can tell all our online friends that we think we just failed an exam. Are these changes good or bad? That's for each person to decide. But one thing is certain—as more people join social networks and as new networks continue to appear, we can expect more changes in the future.

B | Skimming. Now read the whole paragraph carefully. Were you correct about the main idea?

🎧 track 1-08

For many of us, visiting Facebook, Twitter, or other online social networks has become a regular part of our daily activities. However, we may not have noticed the significant ways that social networks have changed our lives. First of all, they have changed the way we get our news. These days, we often only read the news stories that our friends post online. Second, our relationships have changed. Now, it's easier to keep in touch with new friends and find old friends that we haven't seen for a long time. Third, many of us share thoughts with our online friends that we used to keep private. For example, in an instant, we can tell all our online friends that we think we just failed an exam. Are these changes good or bad? That's for each person to decide. But one thing is certain—as more people join social networks and as new networks continue to appear, we can expect more changes in the future.

CT Focus

Make inferences as you read. For example, what can you infer from this sentence about how the writer got news in the past?

Lamu: Tradition and Modernity

▲ Traditional houses are tightly packed on the island town of Lamu, Kenya.

Before Viewing

A | **Guessing Meaning from Context.** You will hear these **bold** words in the video. Discuss the meaning of each one with a partner. Write definitions for the words and phrases.

1. When you visit a different culture, it can have an **influence** on the way you think and the things you do.
2. Lamu is having **economic** problems. There are not a lot of jobs, so people can't earn much money.
3. Culture is **dynamic**. It doesn't stay the same forever.
4. Cultures are always changing, but they usually **retain** their most important **features**. For example, language and religion usually stay the same.

B | **Brainstorming.** Why might a traditional culture want to connect to the Internet and become more modern? Why might they *not* want to? List reasons with a partner.

Reasons for: They can learn about other countries.

_____

Reasons against: _____

_____

While Viewing

A | Watch the video about Lamu. Does it mention any of the things that you listed in exercise **B** above? Circle any items that are mentioned.

B | Read questions 1–3. Think about the answers as you view the video.

1. Why do some people want to make Lamu more modern?
2. What are some people doing to help make Lamu more modern?
3. How does Sheik Ahmad Badawy feel about changes to the culture of Lamu?

After Viewing

A | Discuss answers to questions 1–3 above with a partner.

B | **Critical Thinking: Synthesizing.** Nowadays, we think of social networking as something we do on the Internet. What kind of social networking did people in Lamu do in the past? How did it affect their culture?

_____

A | **Building Vocabulary.** Read the sentences below. Look at the words around the **bold** words to guess their meanings. Then circle the best definition.

1. A lot of companies **advertise** their products on TV and online. They have commercials on TV and small ads on websites.

   a. provide a way for people to buy products online or on television

   b. tell people about something so that they might buy it or use it

2. Often, old friends **contact** each other online, for example, by using social networks.

   a. communicate or meet with someone

   b. ask someone to do something for money

3. Companies these days are trying to be more **environmentally** responsible. For example, some use only electric cars and others use solar power.

   a. relating to a company and the employees of the company

   b. relating to the natural world of land, sea, air, plants, and animals

4. You can do a lot of different things on social networks. You can write a **message** to a friend, you can find old friends, and you can make new friends.

   a. a piece of information or a request that you send to someone

   b. a homework assignment for a class

5. One **positive** effect of social networking is that people can easily find other people with the same interests.

   a. good or helpful

   b. bad or unhelpful

6. A lot of people like **posting** articles and videos on social networks. They want to share them with their friends.

   a. sending information by email to share with other people

   b. making something available to other people on the Internet

7. Texting is a good **tool** for communicating with many friends at the same time.

   a. a website that is used by a lot of people for a particular purpose

   b. something that you use to do a particular thing

Word Link

The suffix **-al** often indicates that a word is an adjective, e.g., virtu**al**, trib**al**, environment**al**, cultur**al**, structur**al**, tradition**al**, influenti**al**, economic**al**.

Word Partners

Use **environmentally** with adjectives, for example, environmentally **responsible**, environmentally **sound**, environmentally **friendly**, environmentally **aware**, and environmentally **sensitive**.

8. Tui Mali is the leader of a **tribe** near Fiji. They live on an island called Vorovoro, and they speak Fijian.

   a. a group of people who do the same type of job and who work together

   b. a group of people who usually live in the same place and share customs, beliefs, language, etc.

9. With some online games, you can have **virtual** cities. The places aren't real; they only exist online.

   a. used to describe an activity or a game that you can either play on a computer or in reality

   b. used to describe an activity or a game that you can only do on the computer

10. In most communities, important decisions are made by **voting**. In many countries, this is how people choose leaders or make laws.

    a. giving your opinion about a decision, usually by marking a paper or raising your hand

    b. finding out information about laws in your community or about people who want to lead the community

B | Using Vocabulary. Answer the questions in complete sentences. Then share your sentences with a partner.

1. What is something that you do that is **environmentally** responsible?

   _____

   _____

2. What might be one **positive** effect of social networking on people's lives?

   _____

   _____

3. What kinds of things do you usually **post** on social networks? If you don't post things, why not?

   _____

   _____

4. How can you use the Internet as a research **tool**?

   _____

   _____

C | Predicting. Skim the reading on pages 52–53. Why do you think the title is "Internet Island"?

   _____

   _____

Internet Island

track 1-09

▲ Ben Keene, co-creator of tribewanted.com, with members of his tribe.

The Idea

A ON JANUARY 14, 2006, Ben Keene received an email that changed his life. The message was from his friend Mark James. The subject line read: "A TRIBE IS WANTED." Keene and James, both 26, wanted to create an Internet start-up.[1] Here was James's new idea: We will create an online community and call it a tribe. We will make decisions about rules with discussions and online voting. Then we will do something that no one has ever done—our virtual tribe will become a real one. We will travel to a remote island and form a partnership with a local tribe. We will build an environmentally friendly community and share it with the world.

B James's idea came from social-networking websites, which got hundreds of millions of visitors a year. People spent a lot of time online, but they spent most of that time posting messages and sharing music. In James's opinion, these sites could be used for so much more.

The Island

C Keene liked the idea, and he and James named their website tribewanted.com. Then they began looking for an island for their tribe. Around the same time, Tui Mali, the chief of a tribe in Fiji, wanted jobs and money for his people. He owned a small island called Vorovoro. The main islands of Fiji were becoming very modern, but Vorovoro was not.

[1] An **Internet start-up** is a newly created online business.
[2] If you **lease** a building or a piece of land, you allow someone to use it in return for regular payments.
[3] **Donations** are money or items that someone gives to an organization to help it.

Vorovoro, Fiji

On Vorovoro, a few people had cell phones or worked on one of the main islands, but most lived in very small, simple homes with no electricity or running water.

Tui Mali wanted to find someone to develop his island. So he decided to advertise his island on the Internet. A few weeks later, Keene and James contacted him. They agreed to pay $53,000 for a three-year lease[2] of the island and $26,500 in donations[3] to the community. They also promised jobs for the local tribe members. "We are all excited about Tribewanted," Tui Mali told a local newspaper reporter. "It will provide us with work for the next three years." Tui Mali was happy to have the money, but he also trusted that Keene and James would respect his culture.

▲ Tribal chief Tui Mali hopes the Tribewanted project will provide jobs and income without destroying his people's land or culture.

The New Tribe

The Internet tribe quickly attracted people. In a few months, it had 920 members from 25 countries. In September of 2006, Keene and 13 of his tribe members, aged 17 to 59, traveled to the island for the first time. (James stayed at home to manage the website.) When they arrived, the local tribe, along with their chief Tui Mali, were there to greet them.

▲ The Vorovoro islanders helped the new arrivals to build a structure for their central meeting place.

For several weeks after the newcomers arrived, they worked with the local tribe members. They built buildings, planted crops behind the village, set up non-polluting sources of energy, such as solar power, and ate fresh fish from the ocean. As they worked together, they became friends. Eventually they became one tribe.

Through the Internet, the tribe connected with almost a thousand people from all over the world. On the island, it brought together groups of people from very different cultures. Keene and Tui believe the new tribal connections will help the island to develop in a positive way. They hope the island will become more modern, without losing its traditional culture.

The Tribe Keeps Growing

Today, Tribewanted continues to use social networking as a tool to connect in a real environment. Anyone can go to the website to join the online tribe, donate money, or plan a visit to Vorovoro. Members can also visit a new location in Sierra Leone. In the next ten years, the creators of the site hope to create more communities across the globe, bringing people and cultures together in a global Internet tribe.

A | **Understanding the Gist.** Look back at your answer to exercise **C** on page 51. Was your prediction correct?

B | **Identifying Main Ideas.** Write the main idea for each of the paragraphs listed below.

1. Paragraph A: _____
_____

2. Paragraph B: _____
_____

3. Paragraph E: _____
_____

4. Paragraph G: _____
_____

Strategy

When you **scan for key details**, first consider what *kind* of information you need to scan for.

C | **Identifying Key Details.** Read the sentences below. What kind of information is missing in each one? Match the kinds of information (a–h) with the sentences (1–8). Then read the passage to complete each sentence.

a. a country name	b. a person's name	c. a type of food	d. a website name
e. a year	f. an adjective	g. an amount of money	h. an island name

_____ 1. _____ sent a message to his friend Ben Keene about starting a tribe.

_____ 2. James and Ben named their online site _____.

_____ 3. They found a small island for their tribe. It's called _____.

_____ 4. They paid _____ to lease the island for three years.

_____ 5. In September _____, Keene went to the island with 13 other people.

_____ 6. The members of the new tribe ate _____ while they lived on the island.

_____ 7. Keene and the tribal leader hope the island will become more _____, but still keep its traditions.

_____ 8. James and Keene started another tribe in _____ in West Africa.

D | **Critical Thinking: Making Inferences.** Write your answers to the questions. Underline the parts of the text that help you answer the questions. Then share your answers with a partner.

1. What kind of people do you think join Tribewanted?
_____

2. What do you think Tribewanted members can learn from the experience of going to Vorovoro? _____
_____

3. How do you think Tribewanted has changed Tui Mali and his tribe members?
_____

GOAL: In this lesson, you are going to plan, write, revise, and edit a paragraph on the following topic: ***Do you think online media such as social networks and blogs have mainly improved our lives, or have they changed our lives in a negative way?***

A | Read the information in the box. Use the present perfect tense of the verbs in parentheses to complete the sentences (1–4).

Language for Writing: The Present Perfect Tense

Use the present perfect tense to talk about something that happened several times in the past, something that happened at an unspecified time in the past, something that began in the past and continues to the present, or when the time in the past is not important. To form the present perfect, use *have* or *has* and the past participle of a main verb.

> I think online media **have improved** our lives.
> Thousands of people **have created** blogs in the past few years.
> We **have used** several different kinds of social networks recently.
> She **has posted** videos on YouTube three times.

Remember to use the simple past to talk about something that happened at a *specific* time in the past (see page 35).

For more explanation and examples, see page 216.

Example: I __have contacted__ (*contact*) all of my classmates on Facebook.

1. Social media _____ (*change*) our lives in many ways.

2. Michael Wesch _____ (*use*) social media in several of his classes.

3. My friend _____ (*meet*) a lot of great people on social networking sites.

4. A lot of old friends _____ (*find*) me online.

B | Write five sentences using the present perfect tense. Write about ways that social media have changed your life, and ways that you have used social media.

C | **Brainstorming.** Brainstorm a list of things that people do with online media.

_____

_____

_____

_____

D | **Journal Writing.** Use your ideas from exercise **C** to write a response in your journal to the following question. Write for three minutes.

How have online media changed the way people communicate with each other?

Writing Skill: *Writing a Concluding Sentence*

Formal paragraphs often have concluding sentences. A concluding sentence is the last sentence of a paragraph. It ties the paragraph together.

Concluding sentences can state an opinion (either the author's, or a person mentioned in the paragraph), make a prediction, or ask a question for the reader to think about. They can also restate, or summarize, the main idea of a long or complex paragraph.

E | Critical Thinking: Analyzing. Find and underline these concluding sentences in the reading passages in this unit. What does each sentence do? Write **Q** (asks a question), **P** (makes a prediction), **O** (gives an opinion), or **R** (restates the main idea).
(Note that sentences may have more than one correct answer.)

Reading A:

___ 1. In fact, Wesch says, "the Web is us."

___ 2. "And yet do any of us really use it for all the potential that's there?"

Reading B:

___ 3. We will build an environmentally friendly community and share it with the world.

___ 4. In James's opinion, these sites could be used for so much more.

___ 5. In the next 10 years, the creators of the site hope to create more communities across the globe . . .

F | Write a concluding sentence for each paragraph below.

1.   Everywhere you look these days, people are on their phones, tablets, or computers. Some are talking, some are texting, and some are surfing the Web. It seems like people communicate with each other on social networks and by email more than they do in person. According to Dan Buettner, in his book *Thrive*, people should spend six to seven hours a day socializing with friends and family in order to increase their happiness. Socializing online probably doesn't have the same effect as socializing in person does.

[Write a prediction.] _____

_____

_____

2.   In my opinion, reading the news online is better than reading a newspaper or watching the news on TV. One way that it is better is that readers can comment on articles that they read online. They can have conversations with other readers, and sometimes even with the writer. Also, online articles provide links to additional information. For example, if an article mentions a name, the name is often linked to another article with more information about that person. Finally, online news articles can be updated if something changes during the day. For example, an online news site might post an article about a dangerous storm in the morning. If more information about the storm becomes available later that day, it can be added to the article.

[Restate the main idea.] _____

_____

_____

A | **Planning.** Follow the steps to make notes for your paragraph. Don't worry about grammar or spelling. Don't write complete sentences.

Step 1: Look at your journal entry from page 55. Underline the positive ways that social networking has changed communication. Circle the negative ways.

Step 2: Decide whether you think online social networking has improved our lives more or harmed us more. Write a topic sentence that states your main idea.

Step 3: Look at your brainstorming notes and journal entry again. Complete the chart.

Outline

Topic: Has online social networking helped us or harmed us?

Topic sentence _____

_____

Supporting Idea
(one way social
networking has helped
or harmed us) _____

_____

Details: _____

Supporting Idea
(another way social
networking has helped
or harmed us) _____

_____

Details _____

_____

Concluding sentence _____

_____

B | **Draft 1.** Use your notes to write a first draft of your paragraph.

Strategy

For an opinion paragraph, you can use these phrases in your topic sentence:

I think . . . I believe . . . In my opinion . . .

You can also use one of them in your concluding sentence if you end the paragraph with a statement of your opinion.

C | Analyzing. The paragraphs below are on the topic of online music sharing.

Which is the first draft? _____   Which is the revision? _____

a There are many views about online music sharing, but in my opinion, people should pay for music instead of getting it free online. I have gotten free music online in the past, and I didn't really think about whether or not it was fair to the musician. Then I thought about how musicians make money. They earn money by giving concerts and selling CDs. I realized that when I get music free online, I'm stealing from the people who made the music. Musicians work hard to write and perform songs. If people want to enjoy those songs, they should pay for them. We don't expect other kinds of professionals to work for free. For example, we don't expect doctors to treat us for free or teachers to teach for free. If musicians don't get paid for their work, they might not be able to continue making music. They might have to find other work in order to make money. Without musicians, where would we get our music?

b There have been a lot of disagreements about online music sharing. I have gotten free music online in the past, and I didn't really think about whether or not it was fair to the musician. Then I thought about how musicians make money. They earn money by giving concerts and selling CDs. I realized that when I get music free online, I'm stealing from the people who made the music. That's when I stopped sharing music online. Now I always pay for music. I feel the same way about sharing movies online. Even though movie studios make millions of dollars, I still don't think it's right to get movies for free. Musicians work hard to write and perform songs. If musicians don't get paid for their work, they might not be able to continue making music. They might have to find other work in order to make money.

CT Focus

Make inferences about the paragraph. What can you tell about the writer? Does he or she use the Internet a lot? Do you think this person is generally honest or dishonest?

D | Analyzing. Work with a partner. Compare the paragraphs above by answering the following questions about each one.

	a	b
1. Does the paragraph have one main idea?	Y N	Y N
2. Does the topic sentence introduce the writer's opinion?	Y N	Y N
3. Does the paragraph include 2–3 supporting ideas?	Y N	Y N
4. Does the paragraph include 1–2 details for each supporting idea?	Y N	Y N
5. Is there any information that doesn't belong?	Y N	Y N
6. Does the paragraph have a concluding sentence or question?	Y N	Y N

E | Revising. Answer the questions in exercise **D** about your own paragraph.

F | Peer Evaluation. Exchange your draft with a partner and follow these steps:

Step 1: Read your partner's paragraph and tell him or her one thing that you liked about it.

Step 2: Complete the chart below with information from your partner's paragraph.

Main Idea	_____
Supporting Idea	_____
Details	_____
Supporting Idea	_____
Details	_____
Concluding sentence	_____

Step 3: Compare your chart with the chart your partner completed on page 57.

Step 4: The two charts should be similar. If they aren't, discuss how they differ.

G | Draft 2. Write a second draft of your paragraph. Use what you learned from the peer evaluation activity, and your answers to exercise **E**. Make any other necessary changes.

H | Editing Practice. Read the information in the box. Then find and correct one present perfect mistake in each of the sentences (1–5).

> In sentences using the present perfect, remember to:
> • use the correct form of *have*.
> • use the correct form of the past participle of the main verb. (Be careful with irregular past participles, such as *be—been, do—done, have—had, see—seen, take—taken*.)

1. The Internet been in existence for several decades now, but we are still discovering creative ways to use it.

2. I wasn't sure that I would connect with many people when I joined a social network, but several people have contact me in the past few months.

3. Now that it's so easy to share videos, millions of people has posted videos online.

4. I have saw that video a few times, and I still think it's fun to watch.

5. Our class is doing research about blogs, and we has visited over 100 different blogs in the past month.

I | Editing Checklist. Use the checklist to find errors in your second draft.

Editing Checklist	Yes	No
1. Are all the words spelled correctly?		
2. Is the first word of every sentence capitalized?		
3. Does every sentence end with the correct punctuation?		
4. Do your subjects and verbs agree?		
5. Is the use of present perfect and other verb tenses correct?		

J | Final Draft. Now use your Editing Checklist to write a final draft of your paragraph. Make any other necessary changes.

UNIT QUIZ

p.42 1. In 2007, fewer than one in 20 people in Sub-Saharan Africa had _____.

p.45 2. In the 1950s, the dominant medium was _____.

p.45 3. Michael Wesch believes that if you change the way that people communicate, you change _____ and _____.

p.48 4. Reading quickly to get the general idea of what a passage is about is called _____.

p.52 5. Ben Keene and Mark James created an online tribe. They got the idea from using _____.

p.52 6. After creating their website and gathering online tribe members, Keene and James turned their _____ tribe into a real one.

p.56 7. The final sentence of a paragraph that ties the paragraph's ideas together is called a(n) _____.

p.59 8. The present perfect form of *be* for the subject *I* is _____.

Deep Trouble

ACADEMIC PATHWAYS

Lesson A: Interpreting visual information
Examining problems and solutions

Lesson B: Understanding graphic information
Reading an interview

Lesson C: Explaining a chart or graph

Think and Discuss

1. What ocean or sea is nearest your home? When was the last time you saw it?

2. Do you eat seafood? If yes, what types do you eat? If no, why not?

▲ A school of barracuda surrounds a diver off New Hanover Island, Papua New Guinea.

Exploring the Theme

Look at the map and read the information. Then discuss the questions.

1. What do the colors of the map show? What kinds of "activity" does this refer to?

2. Which areas have the highest impact, or effect, of human activities?

3. How is human activity affecting, or changing, the four places described? How are the effects similar and different?

Ocean Impact

Human activities are affecting, in some way, all of the world's oceans. These activities include fishing, farming, manufacturing, and offshore gas and oil drilling.

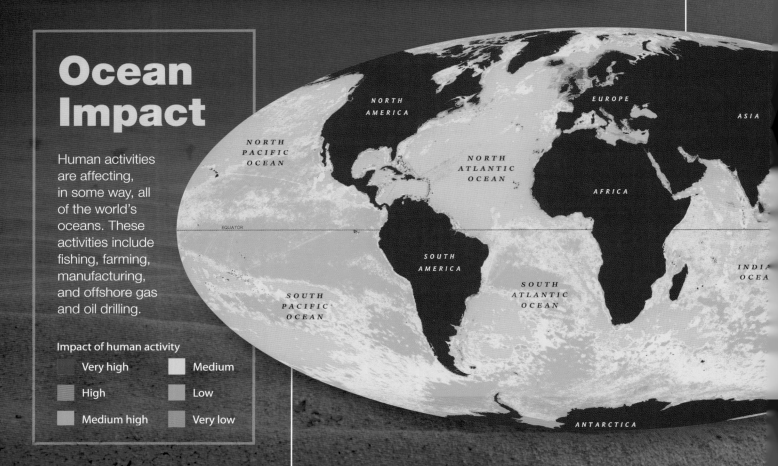

NORTH AMERICA

EUROPE

ASIA

NORTH PACIFIC OCEAN

NORTH ATLANTIC OCEAN

AFRICA

EQUATOR

SOUTH AMERICA

INDIAN OCEAN

SOUTH PACIFIC OCEAN

SOUTH ATLANTIC OCEAN

ANTARCTICA

Impact of human activity

Very high	Medium
High	Low
Medium high	Very low

Caribbean Sea

Pollution and overfishing are causing some fish species to disappear. The temperature of the water is increasing, too. The rising water temperature makes it more difficult for species to survive.

Garbage washes ashore ▶ on the southern edge of Aruba in the Caribbean.

North Sea

Pollution from shipping, farming, and offshore drilling is causing "dead zones"—places without enough oxygen for plants and fish to live. Overfishing adds to the problem.

◀ Pollution from offshore oil and gas drilling is one cause of the North Sea's dead zones.

NORTH
PACIFIC
OCEAN

EQUATOR

AUSTRALIA

East China Sea

Several large rivers bring pollution into the sea. It is also a major fishing area and shipping route. Together, these factors cause serious problems for the ocean environment.

◀ Container ships are a common sight on the rivers that flow from several countries into the East China Sea.

Coral Sea

The Coral Sea has less impact from human activity than other oceans. However, the water is warming and becoming acidic.[1] Plants and fish cannot live in acidic water.

◀ The humphead wrasse is among thousands of fish species living in the Great Barrier Reef in Australia's Coral Sea.

▲ (Main photo) Waves of sand carpet the ocean floor of Australia's Coral Sea.

[1] If something is **acidic**, it contains acid, a chemical that is harmful to the environment.

A | **Building Vocabulary.** Find the words in **blue** in the reading passage on pages 65–66. Read the words around them and try to guess their meanings. Then write the correct word from the box to complete each sentence (1–10).

diverse	ecosystem	estimate	population	quantity
reduce	restore	species	stable	survive

1. If you _____reduce_____ something, you make it less.
2. To _____survive_____ is to continue to live or exist.
3. If something is _____diverse_____, it has things that are very different from each other.
4. A(n) _____species_____ is a group of plants or animals whose members are very similar to each other.
5. A(n) _____quantity_____ is a number or an amount.
6. A(n) _____ecosystem_____ is the relationship between all the plants and animals that live together in a particular area.
7. If you _____restore_____ something, you make it the way it was before.
8. When you _____estimate_____ something's size or number, you make a guess based on the information available.
9. The _____population_____ is the number of people or animals that live in a particular place.
10. Something that is _____stable_____ is not likely to change.

Word Partners

Use **reduce** with nouns: reduce **costs**, reduce **crime,** reduce **spending,** reduce **the number of** (something), reduce **waste**; you can also use **reduce** with adverbs: **dramatically** reduce, **greatly** reduce, **significantly** reduce.

B | **Using Vocabulary.** Answer the questions. Share your ideas with a classmate.

1. What do fish need to **survive**? What do people need to **survive**?
2. How can we **reduce** pollution?
3. Which countries do you think have the largest **populations**? Which cities have the largest **populations**?

C | **Brainstorming.** Make a list of possible problems in the oceans today.

D | **Predicting.** Read the title of the passage on page 65. Then look at the pictures and the captions. What do you think the reading is mainly about?

a. why there are more fish today

b. why there are fewer fish today

c. why the ocean is polluted today

Where Have All the Fish Gone?

▲ A yellow goby looks through the window of its soda can home in Suruga Bay, Japan.

track 1-10

A THROUGHOUT HISTORY, people have thought of the ocean as a diverse and limitless source of food. Yet today there are clear signs that the oceans have a limit. Most of the big fish in our oceans are now gone. One major factor is overfishing. People are taking so many fish from the sea that species cannot replace themselves. How did this problem start? And what is the future for fish?

Source of the Problem

B For centuries, local fishermen caught only enough fish for themselves and their communities. However, in the mid-20th century, people around the world became interested in making protein-rich foods, such as fish, cheaper and more available. In response to this, governments gave money and other help to the fishing industry.

▼ A bottom trawler drags along the ocean floor of Baja California.

C As a result, the fishing industry grew. Large commercial fishing[1] companies began catching enormous quantities of fish for profit and selling them to worldwide markets. They started using new fishing technologies that made fishing easier. These technologies included sonar[2] to locate fish, and dragging large nets along the ocean floor. Modern technology allows commercial fishermen to catch many more fish than local fishermen can.

A thresher shark struggles in a net in the Gulf of California. ▶
An estimated 38 million sharks are caught every year.

[1] **Commercial fishing** is fishing for profit.
[2] **Sonar** technology uses sound waves to locate objects, for example, underwater.

Rise of the Little Fish

D   In 2003, a scientific report estimated that only 10 percent remained of the large ocean fish populations that existed before commercial fishing began. Specifically, commercial fishing has greatly reduced the number of large predatory fish,[3] such as cod and tuna. Today, there are plenty of fish in the sea, but they're mostly just the little ones. Small fish, such as sardines and anchovies, have more than doubled in number—largely because there are not enough big fish to eat them.

E   This trend is a problem because ecosystems need predators to be stable. Predators are necessary to weed out[4] the sick and weak individuals. Without this weeding out, or survival of the fittest, ecosystems become less stable. As a result, fish are less able to survive difficulties such as pollution, environmental change, or changes in the food supply.

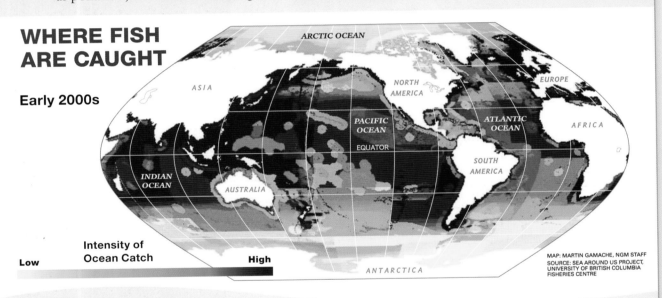

WHERE FISH ARE CAUGHT

Early 2000s

Intensity of Ocean Catch

Low   High

MAP: MARTIN GAMACHE, NGM STAFF
SOURCE: SEA AROUND US PROJECT,
UNIVERSITY OF BRITISH COLUMBIA
FISHERIES CENTRE

A Future for Fish?

F   A study published in 2006 in the journal *Science* made a prediction: If we continue to overfish the oceans, most of the fish that we catch now—from tuna to sardines—will largely disappear by 2050. However, the researchers say we can prevent this situation if we restore the ocean's biodiversity.[5]

G   Scientists say there are a few ways we can do this. First, commercial fishing companies need to catch fewer fish. This will increase the number of large predatory fish. Another way to improve the biodiversity of the oceans is to develop aquaculture—fish farming. Growing fish on farms means we can rely less on wild-caught fish. This gives species the opportunity to restore themselves. In addition, we can make good choices about what we eat. For example, we can stop eating the fish that are the most in danger. If we are careful today, we can still look forward to a future with fish.

---

[3] **Predatory fish** are fish that kill and eat other fish.
[4] **To weed out** is to remove something because it is not good or strong enough.
[5] **Biodiversity** is the existence of a wide variety of plant and animal species.

A | **Understanding the Gist.** Look back at your answer for exercise **D** on page 64. Was your prediction correct?

B | **Guessing Meaning from Context.** Find the following terms in the reading passage on pages 65–66 and circle them. Note the paragraph letter where you find them. Underline the words or phrases that help you understand their meaning. Then write your own definition.

1. **overfishing:** Paragraph: _____ My definition: _____

2. **survival of the fittest:** Paragraph: _____ My definition: _____

3. **aquaculture:** Paragraph: _____ My definition: _____

C | **Identifying Main Ideas.** Answer the following questions using information from the reading passage.

1. What is the main reason that most of the big fish in the oceans are gone now?

   _____

2. Why can the commercial fishing industry catch more fish than local fishermen can?

   _____

3. Why are large populations of little fish a problem?

   _____

4. What might eventually happen if fishing continues at the current rate?

   _____

D | **Critical Thinking: Analyzing.** Discuss these questions with a partner: What is the main problem described in the reading passage on pages 65–66? What possible solutions are there to this problem? Complete the T-chart.

Main Problem	Solutions
	1.
	2.
	3.

> **CT Focus**
>
> In a **problem-solution passage**, a writer usually describes a problem first and then provides possible solutions. As you read, ask yourself: *Does the writer provide enough information to show why the problem is real? Is it clear how the solutions match the problem(s)?*

E | **Critical Thinking: Evaluating Arguments.** Discuss your answers to the following questions about "Where Have All the Fish Gone?"

1. Does the writer provide enough supporting information to show that the problem of overfishing is real? If so, how does he or she do this?

2. How well do the solutions help to address the problem? Has the writer given enough information so the reader can see how they might work?

F | **Personalizing.** Discuss this question with a partner: After reading the passage, do you plan to change any of your eating choices? Why, or why not?

Reading Skill: *Interpreting Visual Information*

Writers use charts, graphs, and maps to show information **visually**; that is, to make information easier to see.

The **title** will help you understand the main idea; that is, what the visual information shows.

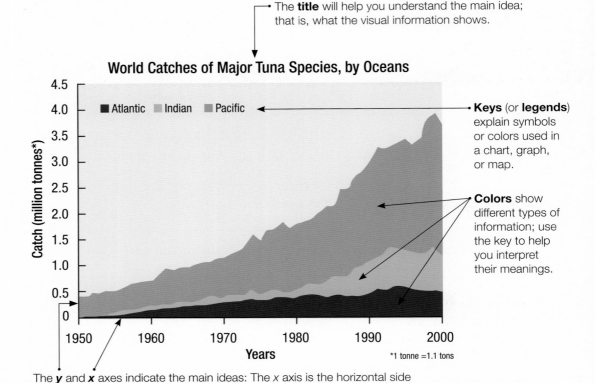

World Catches of Major Tuna Species, by Oceans

Keys (or **legends**) explain symbols or colors used in a chart, graph, or map.

Colors show different types of information; use the key to help you interpret their meanings.

The **y** and **x** axes indicate the main ideas: The *x* axis is the horizontal side of a bar or a line graph. The *y* axis is the vertical side.

Source: United Nations Fisheries and Agricultural Organization (FAO)

👥 **A** | **Interpreting a Graph.** Look at the line graph above and discuss your answers to the questions.

1. What does the line graph show?

2. What does the dark blue color represent?

3. Approximately how many tonnes of tuna were caught in the Indian Ocean in 2000?

B | **Interpreting Maps.** Look at the map on page 66 and answer the questions.

1. What does the map show? What do the colors show?

2. How is the map similar to, and different from, the map on pages 62–63?

👥 **C** | **Critical Thinking: Synthesizing.** Use the map on page 66 and the graph above to answer the following question: In which parts of the world was overfishing a major problem at the end of the 20th century?

Saving Bluefin Tuna

◀ A diver in Tokyo's Sea Life Park reaches out to a passing bluefin tuna, one of the largest and fastest species of fish in the world.

A 1,000 pound (450 kilogram) bluefin ▶ tuna is loaded onto a fishing boat.

Before Viewing

A | **Using a Dictionary.** Here are some words you will hear in the video. Write each word or phrase next to its definition (1–4). Use your dictionary to help you.

> breed   hatchlings
> in captivity   the wild

1. _____: baby fish
2. _____: not free; unable to go where you want
3. _____: have babies
4. _____: a natural environment

B | **Brainstorming.** Look at the video title and read the photo captions. Why might people want to save bluefin tuna? Brainstorm ideas with a partner.

_____

While Viewing

A | Watch the video about saving bluefin tuna. Does it mention any of the things that you brainstormed in exercise **B** above?

B | As you view the video, think about the answers to these questions.

1. How is Shukei Masuma helping the bluefin tuna population grow?
2. Why is Masuma's job difficult?
3. How much has the population of bluefin tuna declined since the 1970s? Where?
4. What other solution is there to help save the bluefin tuna?

After Viewing

A | Discuss answers to the questions 1–4 above with a partner.

B | **Critical Thinking: Synthesizing.** According to the reading on pages 65–66, what else could people do to help solve the bluefin tuna problem?

A | **Building Vocabulary.** Read the definitions below of the words in **blue** in the reading on pages 72–73. Then complete each sentence with the correct word or phrase.

advice (*n.*): an opinion about what someone should do

avoid (*v.*): choose not to do something

declining (*v.*): becoming less

definitely (*adv.*): for sure

essential (*adj.*): extremely important or absolutely necessary

impact (*n.*): an effect

individual (*n.*): a person

informed (*adj.*): based on knowledge or information

minimal (*adj.*): very small

rely on (*v.*): need or depend on someone or something in order to live or exist

Word Link

mini = very small: **mini**mal, **mini**mum, **mini**mize, **mini**ature, **mini**bus

1. Commercial fishing has had a big _____ on the populations of large fish. The numbers of certain fish are declining as a result of this overfishing.

2. A(n) _____ who eats seafood needs to know which fish are disappearing in order to make responsible eating choices.

3. You should _____ doing things that are harmful to the environment.

4. People who catch just enough fish for their own families have only a _____ effect on the ocean's ecosystem.

5. Overfishing has led to _____ populations of predator fish.

6. Protection of declining fish populations is _____ for the health of the oceans. If certain species die out, the ocean's ecosystem will be unbalanced.

7. Larger fish _____ smaller fish to survive. They need the smaller fish for food.

Word Partners

Use the adjective **informed** with nouns: informed **choice**, informed **decision**. Use the verb **inform** with nouns: inform **parents**, inform the **police**, inform **readers**, inform *someone* in writing, inform *someone* of *something*.

8. If you want to make _____ choices about seafood, you can do research online to find out which fish you should eat and which ones you shouldn't.

9. A lot of people want to continue to eat fish, but also protect the ocean, so they need _____ on how to buy and eat fish responsibly.

10. Overfishing is _____ having a negative effect on the ocean's ecosystem. It is destroying some species of fish.

B | Using Vocabulary. Answer the questions in complete sentences. Then share your sentences with a partner.

1. What are three things you think are **essential** for the health of the planet?

2. How do you stay **informed** about environmental issues?

3. Are there any kinds of food that you **avoid**? Why?

4. Does anyone **rely on** you for anything? What do people rely on you for?

C | Brainstorming. Note some ideas about things you can do to help keep the oceans healthy.

stop eating fish with declining populations,

_____

_____

Strategy

Use titles and visuals, such as charts and maps, to predict what a passage will be about.

D | Predicting. Look at the titles and visuals on pages 72–73. Then complete the sentences.

1. I think the interview is about a person who _____.

2. I think the illustration and chart show _____.

An Interview with Barton Seaver

track 1-11

A Barton Seaver is a chef and conservationist[1] who wants our help to save the oceans. He believes that the choices we make for dinner have a direct impact on the ocean's health. According to Seaver, individuals can make a big difference by making informed choices.

Q. *Should people stop eating seafood?*

B People should definitely not stop eating seafood altogether. There are certain species that have been severely overfished and that people should avoid for environmental reasons. But I believe that we can save the oceans while continuing to enjoy seafood. For example, some types of seafood, such as Alaskan salmon, come from well-managed fisheries. And others, such as farmed mussels and oysters, actually help to restore declining wild populations and clean up polluted waters.

Q. *What kind of seafood should people eat?*
What should they not eat?

C My general advice is to eat fish and shellfish that are low on the food chain and that can be harvested[2] with minimal impact on the environment. Some examples include farmed mussels, clams and oysters, anchovies, sardines, and herring. People should not eat the bigger fish of the sea, like tuna, orange roughy, shark, sturgeon, and swordfish.

Q. *Why did you choose to dedicate[3] your life to the ocean?*

D I believe that the next great advance in human knowledge will come not from new discoveries, but rather from learning how we relate to our natural world. Humans are an essential part of nature, yet humans do not have a very strong relationship with the world around them. I have dedicated myself to helping people to understand our place on this planet through the foods that we eat.

Q. *Why do you believe people should care about the health of the oceans?*

E The health of the oceans is directly linked to the health of people. The ocean provides most of the air we breathe. It has a big effect on the weather that we rely on for crops and food production. It also provides a necessary and vital[4] diet for billions of people on the planet. So I don't usually say that I am trying to save the oceans. I prefer to say that I am trying to save the vital things that we rely on the ocean for.

---

[1] A **conservationist** is someone who works to protect the environment.
[2] When you **harvest** something, such as a crop or other type of food, you gather it in.
[3] When you **dedicate** yourself to something, you give it a lot of time and effort because you think it is important.
[4] Something that is **vital** is very important.

LEVEL 4 **TOP PREDAT⬤**
When you eat
1 pound
of a level 4 fish,
it's like eating ...

What We Eat Makes a Difference

LEVEL 4 **TOP PREDATORS**

ATLANTIC BLUEFIN TUNA

The ocean's top predators are the biggest, fastest animals. Some examples are sharks, tuna, orange roughy, and seals. They mostly eat smaller carnivores.

ORANGE ROUGHY

ATLANTIC SALMON

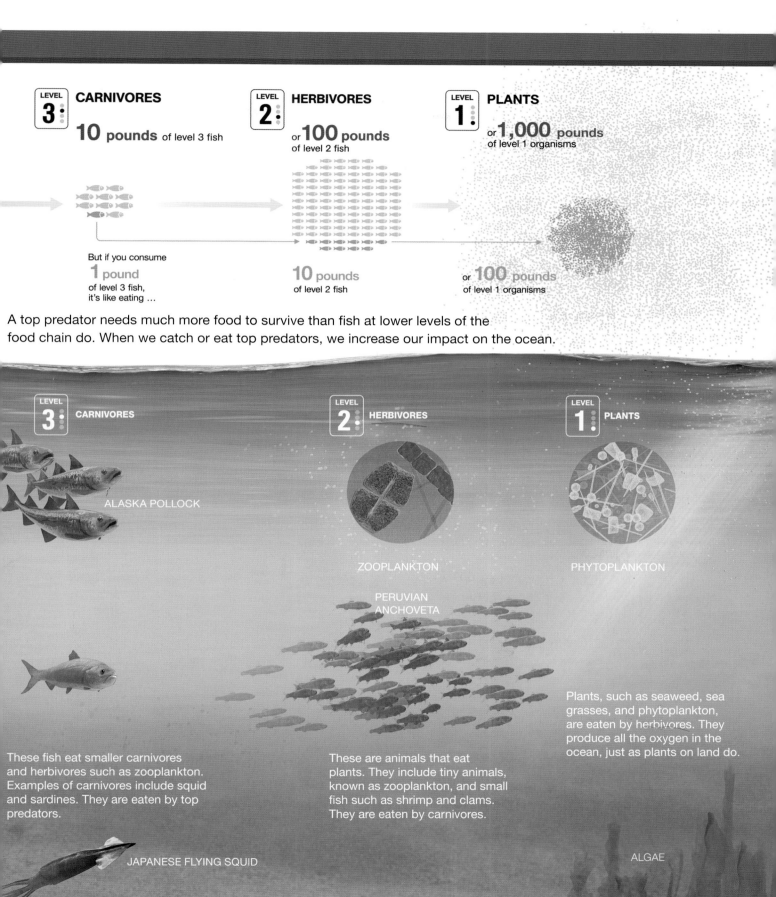

LEVEL 3: CARNIVORES

10 pounds of level 3 fish

LEVEL 2: HERBIVORES

or **100** pounds of level 2 fish

LEVEL 1. PLANTS

or **1,000** pounds of level 1 organisms

But if you consume
1 pound
of level 3 fish,
it's like eating …

10 pounds
of level 2 fish

or **100** pounds
of level 1 organisms

A top predator needs much more food to survive than fish at lower levels of the food chain do. When we catch or eat top predators, we increase our impact on the ocean.

LEVEL 3: CARNIVORES

ALASKA POLLOCK

PERUVIAN ANCHOVETA

These fish eat smaller carnivores and herbivores such as zooplankton. Examples of carnivores include squid and sardines. They are eaten by top predators.

JAPANESE FLYING SQUID

AMERICAN LOBSTER

LEVEL 2: HERBIVORES

ZOOPLANKTON

These are animals that eat plants. They include tiny animals, known as zooplankton, and small fish such as shrimp and clams. They are eaten by carnivores.

LEVEL 1: PLANTS

PHYTOPLANKTON

Plants, such as seaweed, sea grasses, and phytoplankton, are eaten by herbivores. They produce all the oxygen in the ocean, just as plants on land do.

ALGAE

A | Understanding the Gist. What is Barton Seaver's main message in the interview on page 72? Choose the best answer.

a. People should stop eating seafood so the ocean's ecosystem can be restored again.
b. The ocean provides most of the air we breathe and the food we eat.
c. Individuals can have a positive impact on the ocean by making good food choices.

B | Identifying Purpose. Choose the correct answer for each question.

1. What is the purpose of the chart at the top of pages 72–73?
   a. to show how many fish are eaten in one year
   b. to show how our seafood choices impact the ocean's ecosystem

2. What is the purpose of the illustration on pages 72–73?
   a. to illustrate the levels of the ocean food chain, from largest to smallest
   b. to illustrate how some sea animals have become extremely large

C | Identifying Key Details. Use information from pages 72–73 to complete the following sentences.

1. Some examples of herbivores are ____sea shrimpera glasses____
2. Plants are important for the ocean's ecosystem because ____they produce all of oxigon in the oceans.____
3. Eating a pound of orange roughy is like eating ____hundred poond____ of shrimp.
4. Barton Seaver says he works to protect the oceans because ____he believe that choices we make for dinner have direct impact on the oceans health.____

D | Critical Thinking: Analyzing Problems and Solutions. For each problem below, write one or two of Barton Seaver's suggestions that might help solve it.

CT Focus

Examine the problems and solutions in exercise **D**. Do you think each suggestion is an effective solution to each problem? Are the suggestions realistic?

Problems	Suggestions
Some wild fish populations are declining.	1. eat some seafood from farm. 2. not eat some seafood in spawning season.
People don't have a strong relationship with the world around them.	1. include this information in classroom.

E | Critical Thinking: Synthesizing. Discuss the questions in small groups.

1. Barton Seaver recommends that people eat smaller fish. How can this help the ocean's ecosystem?

2. Do you agree with Seaver that "humans do not have a very strong relationship with the world around them"? What are some examples in this unit for or against this idea?

GOAL: In this lesson, you are going to plan, write, revise, and edit an explanatory paragraph. Your topic is: **Explain a chart or graph.**

 A | **Brainstorming.** Brainstorm a list of charts and graphs that you see in your daily life.

_____

_____

B | **Journal Writing.** Write an answer in your journal to the following question. Write for three minutes.

What kinds of information can charts and graphs show?

C | **Analyzing.** Read the information in the box. Use the language in the box and the graph below to complete the sentences (1–4).

Language for Writing: Describing Charts and Graphs

We use certain words to describe information in charts and graphs.

Phrases to introduce a description of a chart or graph:
According to the graph, . . . As the chart shows, . . . We can see from the chart that . . .

Common verbs (usually in simple past)
↑ _rose to / by, increased to / by, doubled (= x2), tripled (= x3), quadrupled (= x4), reached (a low point of / a high point of)_
↓ _declined, decreased, dipped, dropped, fell_
→ _remained stable/steady, stayed (about) the same_

Prepositions

Use _to_ with most verbs to talk about a number or amount that something reached.

Use _by_ with most verbs to talk about how much something changed.

Use these words to talk about time: _over_—a period of time; _between_—a period from one year to another; _by_—at a certain time; _in_—during a number of years.

As the graph shows, _sales_ **rose to** _$50 million_ **by** _2010._

According to the graph, _seafood sales_ **fell by** _20 percent over two years._

As the chart shows, _sales of orange roughy_ **doubled in** _five years._

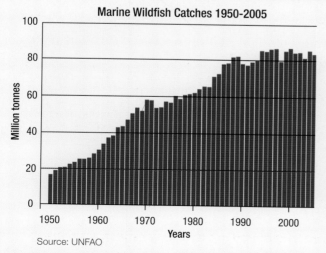

Marine Wildfish Catches 1950-2005

Source: UNFAO

Example: According to the graph, the amount of fish caught ___doubled___ from about 17 million tons (metric tons) in 1950 to about 35 million tons in 1962.

1. The amount of fish caught more than ___quadrupled___ between 1950 and 2005.

2. The amount of fish caught ___increased___ by about 20 million tons between 1980 and 1990.

3. The amount of fish caught ___dropped___ slightly between 1970 and 1972.

4. The amount of fish caught ___remained___ between 1994 and 2004.

D | **Applying.** Write five more sentences about the chart above.

Writing Skill: *Explaining a Chart or Graph*

We usually begin a description of a chart or graph* by explaining its main idea or purpose.

> *According to the chart, eating top predators has a great impact on the ocean's ecosystem.*

> *As the graph shows, the quantity of fish caught has steadily increased since 1950.*

We then provide supporting details—specific data that support the main idea.

> *Eating one pound of a top predator, such as orange roughy, is like eating 10 pounds of a smaller fish, such as herring.*

> *The amount of fish caught between 1950 and 2006 increased from about 17 million metric tons to more than 80 million in 2006.*

*A **graph** usually shows changes over time; a **chart** usually shows numbers or amounts from a single period.

E | Critical Thinking: Analyzing.

Read the sentences about this chart. Check the sentences that are correct. Correct the remaining sentences. Put the five sentences in order to write a paragraph.

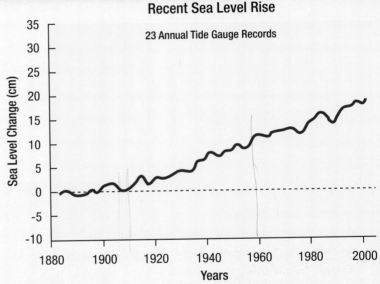

Recent Sea Level Rise

23 Annual Tide Gauge Records

Source: PSMSL, National Oceanography Center, Liverpool, England

☑ 1. According to the graph, sea level rose about 20 centimeters over 120 years.

☑ 2. Sea level rose about 10 centimeters in the 50 years between 1910 and 1960.

☐ 3. After 1910, it began to fall steadily. *(it increased)*

☐ 4. By the year 2000, sea level reached almost 30 centimeters. *(20 centimeters)*

☑ 5. Between 1880 and 1910, it went up and down slightly, but it remained fairly stable.

According to the graph, sea level rose about 20 centimeters over 120 years. Between 1880 and 1910, sea level was stable but after that it increased. Sea level rose about 10 centimeters in 50 years between 1910 and 1960.

A | **Planning.** Follow the steps to make notes for your paragraph.

> **Step 1**   Study the graph on page 68. Decide what the purpose of the graph is.
>
> **Step 2**   Complete the chart below.

Outline

Topic: Describing a Graph

What is the main idea
of the graph?
_____

_____

What is one detail that
supports the main idea
of the graph?
_____

_____

What is another detail
that supports the main
idea of the graph?
_____

_____

What is another detail
that supports the main
idea of the graph?
_____

_____

What is the most recent
piece of data in the graph?
_____

_____

B | **Draft 1.** Use your notes to write a first draft of your paragraph.

C | Analyzing. The paragraphs below describe this graph.

Which is the first draft? _____

Which is the revision? _____

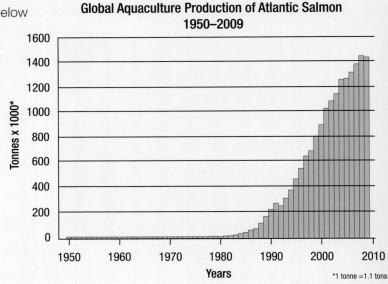

Global Aquaculture Production of Atlantic Salmon 1950–2009

Tonnes x 1000*

*1 tonne =1.1 tons

Years

a According to the graph, farming of Atlantic salmon began in the 1950s and grew quickly in the next 50 years. Between 1980 and 1985, production of Atlantic salmon rose. But around 1985, production began to increase significantly. It rose from about 40 metric tons in 1985 to over 200 in just five years. In the early 1990s, production fell slightly. But then it rose again in 1995. It continued to rise to the year 2000 and beyond. By 2009, production of Atlantic salmon reached almost 1.5 million metric tons. Some people believe that it's better to eat wild salmon, but in my opinion, it's better for the ocean for people to eat farmed salmon.

b According to the graph, farming of Atlantic salmon started to become popular in the 1980s, and after a slow start, it grew quickly. Between 1980 and 1985, production of Atlantic salmon rose slightly. Around 1985, production began to increase more significantly. It rose from about 40,000 metric tons in 1985 to over 200,000 in just five years. Production fell slightly between 1991 and 1992, but then it rose again in 1993. It continued to rise to the year 2000 and beyond. By 2009, production of Atlantic salmon reached almost 1.5 million metric tons.

D | Critical Thinking: Analysis. Work with a partner. Compare the paragraphs above by answering the following questions about each one.

	a		b	
1. Does the paragraph have one main idea?	Y	N	Y	N
2. Does the topic sentence introduce the purpose of the graph?	Y	N	Y	N
3. Does the paragraph include at least three details that support the main idea of the graph?	Y	N	Y	N
4. Is there any information that is incorrect or doesn't belong?	Y	N	Y	N
5. Does the paragraph include correct phrases, verbs, and prepositions to explain charts and graphs?	Y	N	Y	N
6. Does the concluding sentence give information about the most recent data in the graph?	Y	N	Y	N

E | Revising. Answer the questions above about your own paragraph.

F | Peer Evaluation. Exchange your first draft with a partner and follow these steps.

Step 1   Read your partner's paragraph and tell him or her one thing that you liked about it.

Step 2   Complete the chart below with information from your partner's paragraph.

Outline

Topic: Describing a Graph

What is the main idea of the graph? _____

_____

What is one detail that supports the main idea? _____

_____

What is another detail that supports the main idea? _____

_____

What is another detail that supports the main idea? _____

_____

What is the most recent piece of data in the graph? _____

_____

Step 3   Compare your chart with the chart your partner completed on page 77.

Step 4   The two charts should be similar. If they aren't, discuss how they differ.

G | Draft 2. Write a second draft of your paragraph. Use what you learned from the peer evaluation activity, and your answers to exercise **E**. Make any necessary changes.

H | Editing Practice. Read the information in the box. Then find and correct the language mistakes in the sentences below (1–4) that describe the graph on page 78. One of the sentences does not have a mistake.

> In sentences describing a chart or graph, remember to:
> - use the correct prepositions, for example, *between*, *by*, and *in*.
> - use the simple past tense when you are describing data from the past.

1. Between 1991 and 1992, production of Atlantic salmon decline slightly.
2. Production of Atlantic salmon doubled by 1990 and 1995.
3. Production of Atlantic salmon rose steadily between 2000 and 2005.
4. Production of Atlantic salmon increased by about 1.4 million tonnes by 30 years.

I | Editing Checklist. Use the checklist to find errors in your second draft.

Editing Checklist	Yes	No
1. Are all the words spelled correctly?		
2. Is the first word of every sentence capitalized?		
3. Does every sentence end with the correct punctuation?		
4. Do your subjects and verbs agree?		
5. Did you use the past tense to describe changes in the past?		
6. Did you use the correct prepositions and language for describing a graph?		

J | Final Draft. Now use your Editing Checklist to write a third draft of your paragraph. Make any other necessary changes.

UNIT QUIZ

p.62
1. Fishing and offshore drilling are examples of _____ impact _____ that are affecting the world's oceans.

p.64
2. All the living plants and living creatures in a particular area together make up a(n) _____ eco system _____.

p.65
3. Most of the big fish in the ocean are gone because of _____ over fishing _____.

p.68
4. The horizontal and vertical lines on a graph are called the _____ visually _____.

p.72
5. According to Barton Seaver, the health of the oceans is linked to the health of _____ the world _____.

p.73
6. Plants in the ocean are important because they produce all the _____ Oxigen _____ in the sea.

p.75
7. Another way to say something stayed about the same is to say it remained _____ stable _____ or _____ steady _____.

p.76
8. When we write paragraphs about charts and graphs, the topic sentence usually tells the _____ main idea _____ or _____ purpose _____ of the chart or graph.

Memory and Learning

5

Think and Discuss

1. Do you remember what you did on your last birthday? How about your birthday five years ago? Ten years ago?

2. Do you know anyone with a good memory? Why do you think some people can remember things better than others?

▲ As memories fade with age, photographs provide a continuing link with a person's past.

▲ A variety of offerings are left each year by visitors to a war memorial in Maryland, USA.

A. Look at the photo for 30 seconds and answer the questions.

1. How many items can you remember? Close your book and make a list.
2. Compare lists with a classmate. Were some items easier to remember than others?

B. Read the information on this page and discuss these questions with a partner.

1. What are some examples of short-term and long-term memories? What are your earliest long-term memories?
2. What does the chart show about how memory changes with age?

How We Remember

Memory is how the brain stores and recalls information. We make memories when connections are made in the brain's nerve cells, or neurons. Each neuron sends and receives messages. As your eyes scan these pages, billions of **neurons** are working, forming new connections and new memories.

Memories about childhood and things that happened long ago are called **long-term memories**. Telephone numbers and the names of people that we just met are stored in our brains as **short-term memories**.

▲ There are one hundred billion (**100,000,000,000**) nerve cells, or neurons, in the human brain.

Why We Forget

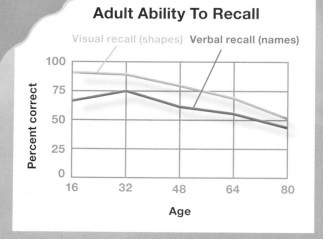

Adult Ability To Recall

Visual recall (shapes)   Verbal recall (names)

Percent correct: 100, 75, 50, 25, 0

Age: 16, 32, 48, 64, 80

Most people have no memory of their childhood before the age of three or four (this is called *childhood amnesia*). We still don't know exactly why—it may be because our brains are not yet fully developed at such a young age. From our teenage years, our ability to remember—or recall—things declines over time, as connections between neurons weaken.

A | Building Vocabulary. Find the words in **blue** in the reading on pages 85–86. Read the words around them and try to guess their meanings. Then write the correct form of each word or phrase next to its definition.

1. _____ (*noun*) a special way of doing a particular thing
2. _____ (*noun*) someone with a very high level of intelligence
3. _____ (*noun*) knowledge that all members of a group share
4. _____ (*verb*) to form a picture in your mind of someone
   or something
5. _____ (*verb*) to learn something so you remember it exactly
6. _____ (*adj.*) inside of something
7. _____ (*adj.*) outside of something
8. _____ (*adj.*) having many different parts; difficult to understand
9. _____ (*noun*) something that is done successfully
10. _____ (*noun*) a book or other written or printed work

> **Word Link**
>
> The suffix **-ize** forms verbs that mean to cause or become something, e.g., *visualize*, *memorize*, *internalize*, *minimize*.

B | Using Vocabulary. Answer the questions. Share your ideas with a partner.

1. What is an example of **collective knowledge**? _____
2. Name one person who you think is a **genius**. _____
3. What **external** conditions can make it difficult to study? _____

C | Classifying. Do you ever make lists to remember things? Do you ever try to *memorize* things? Complete the T-chart below. Compare your answers with a partner's.

Things I make lists for	Things I try to memorize

> **Strategy**
>
> **Scanning** for repeated words can help you predict what a passage is about.

D | Predicting. Scan the reading passage on pages 85–86 quickly. List two other nouns or verbs that appear two or more times.

___memory___   _____   _____

Now look at the words you wrote. What do you think the passage is about?

I think the passage is about _____

_____.

The Art of Memory

track 1-12

A WE ALL TRY TO REMEMBER certain things in our daily lives: telephone numbers, email addresses, facts that we learn in class, important tasks. But did you know that people once had great respect[1] for memory?

B People began to value memory as a skill about 2,500 years ago. That's when the poet Simonides of Ceos discovered a powerful technique known as the loci[2] method. Simonides realized that it's easier to remember places and locations than it is to remember lists of names, for example. According to the loci method, if you think of a very familiar place, and visualize certain things in that place, you can keep those things in your memory for a long time.

▲ A young Ukrainian man attends a service to remember soldiers who died in World War II. Remembrance services play an important role in shaping a society's collective knowledge of the past.

C Simonides called this imagined place a "memory palace." Your memory palace can be any place that you know well, such as your home or your school. To use the loci method to remember a list of tasks, for example, visualize yourself walking through your house. Imagine yourself doing each task in a different room. Later, when you want to remember your list of tasks, visualize yourself walking through your house again. You will remember your list of tasks as you see yourself performing each one.

D Nearly 2,000 years later, a man in 15th-century Italy named Peter of Ravenna used the loci method to memorize books and poems. He memorized religious texts, all of the laws of the time, 200 speeches, and 1,000 poems. By using the loci method, he was able to reread books stored in the "memory palaces" of his mind. "When I [travel] I can truly say I carry everything I own with me," he wrote.

Peter of Ravenna (c. 1448–1508) ▶

[1] If you **respect**, or **have respect for**, something or someone, you have a very high opinion of it or them.
[2] **Loci** is the plural form of the Latin noun *locus*, meaning "place."

When Simonides and Peter of Ravenna were alive, books and pens were not widely available for people to write notes with, so people had to remember what they learned. Mary Carruthers is the author of *The Book of Memory*, a study of the role of memory techniques in the past. She writes, "Ancient and medieval[3] people reserved their awe for memory." In other words, these people thought that a genius was a person with excellent memory. They considered memory to be an art and a great virtue[4] because a person with a good memory could turn external knowledge into internal knowledge.

After Simonides' discovery of the loci method, others continued to develop the art of memory. Memorization gained a complex set of rules and instructions. Students of memory learned what to remember and techniques for how to remember it. In fact, there are long traditions of memory training in many parts of the world. In some cultures, memorization of religious texts is considered a great achievement; many other societies value storytellers who can retell myths and folktales from the past.

But over the past millennium,[5] many things have changed. We've gradually replaced our internal memory with external memory. We've invented technological crutches[6] so we don't have to store information in our brains. We have photographs to record our experiences, calendars to keep track of our schedules, books (and now the Internet) to store our collective knowledge, and note pads—or iPads—for our ideas. By using these crutches, we don't have to remember anything anymore. When we want to know something, we look it up. We've gone from remembering everything to remembering very little. How does this affect us and our society? Did we lose an important skill?

Adapted from "Remember This" by Joshua Foer, *National Geographic Magazine*, Nov 2007

▲ Roman philosopher Seneca the Elder could repeat up to 2,000 names in the order that he heard them.

▼ In Senegal and other parts of West Africa, historians known as *griots* memorize and pass on long stories through poetry, song, and music.

[3] **Medieval** refers to the period of European history between approximately AD 500 and 1500.
[4] A **virtue** is a very good personal quality.
[5] A **millennium** is a period of one thousand years.
[6] A **crutch** is something that someone depends on for support or help

A | Understanding the Gist. Look back at your answer for exercise **D** on page 84. Was your prediction correct?

B | Identifying Key Details. Write answers to the questions.

1. Why did ancient and medieval people think memory was an art?

_____

_____

2. How does the loci method work? Explain the method in your own words.

_____

_____

C | Critical Thinking: Applying a Method. Imagine you have these problems. How might you solve them by using the loci method?

1. You are learning a foreign language. You are having trouble remembering new words.
2. You are taking a history class. It's hard for you to remember when important events happened.

CT Focus

Applying information in a new way can help you internalize it more easily. For example, using the loci method yourself will help you understand and remember how it works.

D | Classifying. Complete the T-chart using information from the reading on pages 85–86. Write techniques, uses, or names related to internal and external memory.

Internal Memory	External Memory
loci method	

E | Critical Thinking: Inferring Opinion. Look at the final paragraph of the reading passage. How might the author answer the question "Did we lose an important skill?" Why do you think so? Discuss your ideas with a partner.

F | Personalizing. Complete the sentences with your own ideas.

1. I think internal memory is better for remembering _____.
2. I think external memory is better for remembering _____.
3. I (think / don't think) we lost an important skill. I think _____

_____.

Reading Skill: *Identifying Cause and Effect*

A **cause** is something that makes another event happen. The resulting event is the **effect**. Recognizing causes and effects can help you better understand a reading passage. Look at the sentence from the reading. Does the underlined portion show a cause or an effect?

> *If you think of a very familiar place, and visualize certain things in that place,*
> <u>*you can keep those things in your memory for a long time*</u>*.*

The underlined portion shows the effect. Visualizing things within a familiar place is the cause. Keeping memories for a long time is the effect.

You can sometimes identify cause and effect relationships by finding certain connecting or signal words. These include *because, so, if, then, therefore, as a result,* and *by* verb + *-ing*.

> *We don't have to remember phone numbers now* **because** *we can store them on smartphones.*

> *I enter my email password three times a day,* **so** *I remember it easily.*

A | **Analyzing.** Read the information about memory techniques. How many cause-effect relationships can you find? Circle the causes and underline their effects.

MEMORY TRICKS

track **1-13**

Techniques for remembering things like lists, numbers, and facts, are called mnemonic devices. For example, people often use things like poems, pictures, or movements because it is easier to remember rhymes, images, or actions than plain facts and lists.

Acronyms are one type of mnemonic. For example, it may be hard to remember the colors of the rainbow in the order that they appear. Someone therefore made an acronym for this: ROY G BIV. The first letters in the acronym are the first letters in the names for the colors: red, orange, yellow, green, blue, indigo, and violet. The name Roy G. Biv is meaningless, but it's short, so it is easier to remember than the list.

English spelling rules can also be difficult to learn, so some students use rhymes to help them remember the rules. By learning "*i* before *e* except after *c* (where you hear *ee*)," students of English remember the spelling of words like *niece* and *receipt*.

▲ Rainbow over Snares Island, New Zealand

CT Focus

Apply this information to words you know. Think of other words that have *ie* or *ei*. Do those words follow the spelling rule?

B | **Analyzing.** Look back at the reading on pages 85–86. Circle three causes and underline their effects.

Memory School

▲ A taxi cab reflects London's famous landmark Westminster Abbey.

Before Viewing

A | **Meaning from Context.** You will hear these phrases in the video. Discuss the meaning of each one with a partner. Write definitions for the words in **bold**.

1. ". . . scientists are studying how the brain is able to **adapt** when it has to **retain** large amounts of information"
2. ". . . **visual processing** takes up more space in the brain than all the other senses combined"
3. ". . . drivers **navigate** the streets of London using a complex **mental map** with thousands of **landmarks** and other locations"

B | **Brainstorming.** When you arrive in a new city, what do you do to become familiar with the streets and find your way around? Make a list with a partner.

use a GPS _____ _____ _____

While Viewing

A | Watch the video about a London driving school. Does it mention any of the things that you listed in exercise **B** above? Circle any items that are mentioned.

B | As you watch the video, think about the answers to these questions.

1. What kinds of things do the taxi drivers do to memorize locations in London?
2. According to the video, what is an important part of preparing for the exam? Why?
3. How do scientists think studying taxi drivers' brains can help other people?
4. What other activities like the London taxi training might enlarge the hippocampus?

After Viewing

A | Discuss answers to the questions 1–4 above with a partner.

B | **Critical Thinking: Synthesizing.** The London taxi drivers' technique and the loci method both involve locations. Discuss with a partner how each technique uses locations.

A | **Building Vocabulary.** Read the sentences below. Look at the words around the **bold** words to guess their meanings. Then circle the best definition.

1. Exercise can **affect** the body in a good way: it can make you healthier.

    a. to make something change in a certain way

    b. to make something bigger

2. People change their **diet** in order to gain or lose weight.

    a. the kinds of food a person normally eats

    b. the times at which a person normally eats

3. Scientists often give a rat a **drug** to make it go to sleep or wake up.

    a. a chemical

    b. an exercise

4. Using the brain in a **mental activity**—such as reading or doing puzzles—can improve memory.

    a. an activity that uses and exercises the mind

    b. an activity that is extremely difficult

5. You need to be in good **physical** condition in order to be a long-distance runner.

    a. relating to the body

    b. relating to money

6. Because of a recent study, we now have **proof** that sleep is important for memory.

    a. information that causes people to disagree

    b. information that shows that something is true

7. A rat learned how to get from one place to another. However, the next day, it got lost because it completely forgot the **route**.

    a. a game

    b. a path

8. If someone is in a **state** of confusion, they are not sure what is happening.

    a. a person's condition at a certain time

    b. a person's hope for the future

Word Partners

Use **stress** with: (*n.*) **effects of** stress, **work-related** stress; (*adj.*) **emotional** stress, **mental** stress, **physical** stress; (*v.*) **cause** stress, **cope with** stress, **deal with** stress, **experience** stress, **reduce** stress.

9. If a student has a lot of **stress** in his or her life, for example, because of problems at school, it might make learning much harder.

   a. a feeling of worry that is caused by difficulties in your life

   b. an illness or a disease that makes it difficult to remember things

10. Taking notes helps you **transfer** information from internal to external memory. This can help you to remember it better.

    a. to move something from one place to another

    b. a study of something that helps people learn about it

> **Word Link**
>
> The prefix **trans-** means "moving across or changing from one thing to another," e.g., **trans**fer, **trans**ition, **trans**late, **trans**form.

B | Using Vocabulary. Answer the questions in complete sentences. Then share your sentences with a partner.

1. What are some ways that you deal with **stress** in your life?

   _____

   _____

> **Top 5 Causes of Stress for College Students**
>
> 1. Finances
> 2. Academic pressure
> 3. Time management
> 4. Roommate conflicts
> 5. Relationships
>
> Source: www.collegeandfinance.com

2. What **routes** do you remember best?

   _____

   _____

3. Do you ever stay up all night to study for a test? How do you think this might **affect** your memory?

   _____

C | Predicting. Underline the key words in the titles and the subheads of the reading passages on pages 92–93. Use the words to help you complete the sentences.

1. I think the reading passage on page 92 is about how _____

   _____

2. I think the reading passage on page 93 is about how _____

   _____

> **Strategy**
>
> **Use key words** in titles and subheads to help you predict what a passage is about.

track **1-14**

NEWSWATCH

Train Your Brain!

Is there anything you can do to have a better memory? Research shows that mental and physical exercise and lifestyle choices can affect memory. In fact, many experts agree it is possible to improve your memory. Here are some tips:

Avoid stress

Recent research shows that stress is bad for the brain. In fact, one study connects worrying with memory loss. Therefore, if you can avoid stress in your life, you may also improve your memory. Relaxation techniques like yoga are one way to reduce stress.

Play games

Can brainteasers[1] like sudoku puzzles improve memory? Some scientists say that mental activity might help memory. Puzzles, math problems, even reading and writing, can probably all benefit the brain.

Get some rest

"Poor sleep before or after learning makes it hard to encode[2] new memories," says Harvard University scientist Robert Stickgold. One study shows that by getting a good night's sleep, people remember a motor skill (such as piano playing) 30 percent better.

Read more about the connection between sleep and memory.

Eat right

Your brain can benefit from a healthy diet, just like the rest of your body. Foods that have antioxidants,[3] such as blueberries, are good for brain cells. This helps memory.

[1] **Brainteasers** are activities that exercise the mind, such as puzzles.
[2] If you **encode** information, you put it into a different form or system of language.
[3] **Antioxidants** are chemicals that can reduce the effect of harmful substances in your body.

Sleep and Memory

Many people think that sleep must be important for learning and memory, but until recently there was no proof. Scientists also believe the hippocampus plays a role in making long-term memories, but they weren't sure how. Now they understand how the process happens—and why sleep is so important.

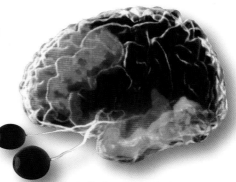

▲ During sleep, ripples travel from the hippocampus (dark purple in this scan) to outer parts of the brain, such as the prefrontal cortex (red).

Memories in Motion

A research team at Rutgers University recently discovered a type of brain activity that happens during sleep. The activity transfers new information from the hippocampus to the neocortex. The neocortex stores long-term memories. The researchers call the transferring activity "sharp wave ripples," because the transferring activity looks like powerful, short waves. The brain creates these waves in the hippocampus during the deepest levels of sleep.

The Rutgers scientists discovered the wave activity in a 2009 study using rats. They trained the rats to learn a route in a maze. Then they let the rats sleep after the training session. They gave one group of sleeping rats a drug. The drug stopped the rats' wave activity. As a result, this group of rats had trouble remembering the route. The reason? The new information didn't have a chance to leave the hippocampus and go to the neocortex.

▼ At night we cycle through different levels, or stages, of sleep. Scientists believe long-term memories are formed during the deepest levels.

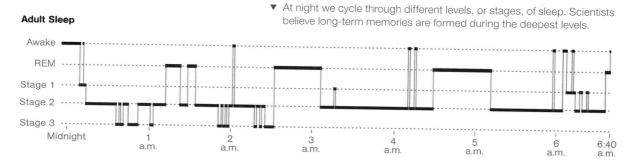

Adult Sleep

Lifelong Memories

The experiment explains how we create long-term memories. The wave activity transfers short-term memories from the hippocampus to the neocortex. Then the neocortex turns the sharp wave ripples into long-term memories. Researcher György Buzsaki says this is "why certain events may only take place once in the waking state and yet can be remembered for a lifetime."

The Rutgers study is important because it proves the importance of sleep for learning and memory. It also finally explains how the brain makes long-term memories.

A | Understanding the Gist. Look back at your answers for exercise **C** on page 91. Were your predictions about the two reading passages correct?

B | Identifying Key Ideas. Work with a partner. Check the things that can improve memory, according to the first reading "Train Your Brain!"

_____ antioxidants   _____ exercise   _____ fatty foods   _____ puzzles

_____ sleep   _____ stress

C | Understanding the Main Idea. What did you learn from the second reading "Sleep and Memory"? Work with a partner to complete this sentence:

The main idea of "Sleep and Memory" is _____

_____

> **Strategy**
>
> **Use key words** in questions, especially nouns and noun phrases, to help you scan for the most relevant parts of a text.

D | Restating Key Details. Complete the following sentences about "Sleep and Memory."

1. A team from Rutgers University found _____

_____.

2. Sharp wave ripples transfer information from the _____

to the _____.

3. Some rats had trouble remembering a route because _____

_____.

E | Matching Cause and Effect. Match the cause with the effect (**a–c**) mentioned in the first reading.

Cause   **Effect**

stres _____   a. forgetting things   b. getting too much sleep   c. avoiding exercise

Now find two cause-effect relationships in the second reading. Circle the causes and underline their effects.

F | Critical Thinking: Synthesizing. Discuss these questions in small groups:

1. List all the methods and tips for improving memory that you learned about in this unit. Circle ones you think you are most likely to use.

the loci method   _____   _____

_____   _____   _____

2. What do people know now about memory that people in the past did not know?

GOAL: In this lesson, you are going to plan, write, revise, and edit a paragraph on the following topic: **What can a person do to improve his or her memory?**

A | **Brainstorming.** Look back at your list for exercise **F** on page 94. Work with a partner. Can you think of any other ways a person could improve their memory? Add ideas to your list.

B | **Journal Writing.** Write an answer in your journal to the following question. Write for three minutes. *What are some ways to improve your memory?*

C | Read the information in the box. Use *by* + gerund to combine the sentence parts (1–3).

Language for Writing: Using *By* + Gerund

Use *by* with a gerund to say how to do something. *By* + gerund forms can appear at the beginning or at the end of a sentence. Use a comma when they appear at the beginning of a sentence.

You can improve your memory **by getting** *enough sleep.*

By getting *enough sleep, you can improve your memory.*

By + gerund expresses how to reach a result:

By eating right, *you can improve your memory.*

    cause   effect

For more explanation and examples, see page 217.

Example: get a good night's sleep / you help your brain form memories

By getting a good night's sleep, you help your brain form memories.

1. write new words on cards / a person can retain them better

   _____

2. give rats drugs / the scientists stopped their brain waves

   _____

3. you can improve your memory / do puzzles

   _____

D | Write five more sentences using *by* + gerund.

Writing Skill: *Using an Outline*

Using an outline helps you to organize your main idea, supporting ideas, and examples and/or details. The examples might be a list of reasons, or steps in a process. An outline is like a map because it gives you something to follow. For example, you can use an outline to develop your ideas in a descriptive paragraph.

Don't write complete sentences in an outline, except for your topic sentence.

E | Matching. Look at the outline below and read the paragraph that follows. Match sentences in the paragraph (a–i) to the parts of the outline. (Two sentences are extra.)

Topic

Topic sentence _____

Supporting Idea 1

Details

Supporting Idea 2

Details

How to Memorize a Route

_____

memorize as steps _____

write names, directions _____

repeat _____

create mental picture _____

study a map _____

imagine following route _____

a. When you have to memorize a route, you should use a technique that works well for you. b. One way is to memorize the directions as a set of steps. c. To do this, write the street names and directions in the correct order on a piece of paper. For example, Step 1 might be: "Drive three miles down Main Street." Step 2 might be: "Turn right on Oak Street." d. If you repeat the steps several times, you won't have to look at the list anymore. e. You can also memorize a route by creating a mental picture of it. f. That is, see the streets and the places on the streets in your mind. g. To do this, study the route as it appears on a map. h. Then imagine yourself following the route. See the buildings and other places along the route in your mind. Turn your body to the right and to the left as you make the turns. By seeing the route in your mind, you will learn it faster. i. There are other ways to learn routes; use the method that works best for you.

F | Critical Thinking: Analyzing. Look again at the two sentences that didn't match the outline. What functions do they have in the paragraph? Match each one to a description:

_____ uses paraphrasing to explain an idea   _____ provides a concluding statement

G | Find and underline two cause-effect relationships in the paragraph.

A | **Planning.** Follow the steps to complete an outline for your paragraph.

Step 1 From your brainstorming notes on page 95, choose your best two or three supporting ideas and write them in the outline below. Don't write complete sentences.

Step 2 Write a topic sentence that introduces your supporting ideas.

Step 3 Now write two examples or details for each supporting idea.

Outline

Topic: How to Improve Your Memory

Topic Sentence _____

Supporting Idea 1 _____

    A. _____

    B. _____

Supporting Idea 2 _____

    A. _____

    B. _____

Supporting Idea 3 _____

    A. _____

    B. _____

B | **Draft 1.** Use your outline to write a first draft. Think about the following questions as you write:

1. Does your paragraph have one main idea?
2. Does your topic sentence introduce your main idea?
3. Do you have 2–3 different supporting ideas?
4. Do you have at least two examples or details for each supporting idea?
5. Is there any information that doesn't belong?
6. Do you have sentences that show cause and effect? Are you using *by* + gerund forms?
7. Are you able to include new vocabulary you have learned in this unit?

C | **Analyzing.** The paragraphs below are on the topic of how people can keep lasting memories.

Which is the first draft? _____   Which is the revision? _____

a One way to record important events in life is to keep a journal. A journal is a written record of events, activities, and thoughts. You can keep a daily journal or an occasional journal. You can write it by hand in a notebook, or type it on a computer. You can also include pictures. Another way to create lasting memories is to use a video journal. With a video journal, you can record activities and events as they are happening. You can make additional recordings afterwards of yourself talking about your thoughts on the events or activities. My phone has a video recorder, but sometimes it doesn't work very well.

b There are two main ways to record the important events in life so that they will become lasting memories. One way is to keep a written journal. This is a written record of events, activities, and thoughts. You can keep a daily journal or an occasional journal. You can write it by hand in a notebook, or type it on a computer. You can also include pictures in your journal. It's a good idea to add text to your photos as a reminder of the places and the people in the photos. Another way to create lasting memories is to use a video journal. With a video journal, you can record activities and events as they are happening. You can also make recordings afterwards of yourself talking about your thoughts on the events or activities. These are just a few of the ways to create lasting memories that you will enjoy for many years.

D | **Critical Thinking: Analysis.** Work with a partner. Compare the paragraphs above by answering the following questions about each one.

	a		b	
1. Does the paragraph have one main idea?	Y	N	Y	N
2. Does the topic sentence introduce the main idea?	Y	N	Y	N
3. Are there two different supporting ideas?	Y	N	Y	N
4. Are there at least two examples for each supporting idea?	Y	N	Y	N
5. Is there any information that doesn't belong?	Y	N	Y	N
6. Is there a concluding sentence?	Y	N	Y	N

CT Focus

Apply these criteria to another paragraph in this Unit, e.g. the final paragraph on p. 86.

E | **Revising.** Answer the questions above about your own paragraph.

F | Peer Evaluation. Exchange your first draft with a partner and follow these steps:

Step 1 Read your partner's paragraph and tell him or her one thing that you liked about it.

Step 2 Write an outline of your partner's paragraph in the space below.

Outline

Topic: How to Improve Your Memory

Topic Sentence _____

Supporting Idea 1 _____

    A. _____

    B. _____

Supporting Idea 2 _____

    A. _____

    B. _____

Supporting Idea 3 _____

    A. _____

    B. _____

Step 3: Compare your outline with the outline that your partner completed on page 97.

Step 4: The two outlines should be similar. If they aren't, discuss how they differ.

G | Draft 2. Write a second draft of your paragraph. Use what you learned from the peer evaluation activity, and your answers to exercise **E**. Make any other necessary changes.

H | Editing Practice. Read the information in the box. Then find and correct one *by* + gerund mistake in each of the sentences (1–4).

When you look for mistakes with *by* + gerund, remember to:

- use the *-ing* form of the verb.
- use a comma when the *by* + gerund form appears at the beginning of a sentence.

---

1. You can't remember all of the information by just listen to a lecture.
2. By take notes while you listen, you can remember information better.
3. By doing a motor activity while you listen you can improve your memory.
4. By write a summary of your notes after a lecture, you will remember the information more easily.

WRITING TASK: Editing

I | Editing Checklist. Use the checklist to find errors in your second draft.

Editing Checklist	Yes	No
1. Are all the words spelled correctly?		
2. Is the first word of every sentence capitalized?		
3. Does every sentence end with the correct punctuation?		
4. Do your subjects and verbs agree?		
5. Are the verb tenses correct?		
6. Did you use *by* + gerund correctly?		

J | Final Draft. Now use your Editing Checklist to write a third draft of your paragraph. Make any other necessary changes.

UNIT QUIZ

p.83 1. We create memories when connections happen in the brain's _____, called neurons.

p.83 2. When you try to remember the name of someone you've just met, you use your _____ memory.

p.84 3. A special way of doing something is called a(n) _____.

p.85 4. Visualizing things arranged in an imagined space is called the _____.

p.86 5. Taking a picture to remember someone is an example of _____ memory.

p.88 6. The underlined part of the sentence below shows the ***cause / effect***.

Because they learned a rhyme, <u>the students were able to remember a new grammar rule.</u>

p.88 7. ROY G BIV is a type of mnemonic called a(n) _____.

p.93 8. The brain creates and stores _____ memories while we are asleep.

Longevity Leaders

UNIT 1

Narrator: The elderly are found across all countries and cultures. And their numbers are increasing as people live longer.

There are over seven billion people in the world today. And this number could reach nine billion by the year 2050. There will be more elderly in the world than ever before.

We will see aging populations all over the world in the 21st century.

Andrew: In places like the United States, Europe, even China, we see populations that are getting much older much faster.

Narrator: But how old is old?

In the natural world, there are animals that live for centuries. Some researchers believe that some whales can live for 200 years or more. Giant tortoises are known to live for 150 years or more. Elephants are known to live for up to 70 years.

Humans live longer than most animals. They can live to a maximum of about 120 years. Of course most humans don't live that long. But there are places in the world where people live longer—and healthier—lives.

This is Sardinia, an island off the coast of Italy. It has a very high number of centenarians. These are people who live to see their 100th birthday. One example is Antonio Bruno, who was still healthy and happy at 103 years old.

National Geographic magazine writer Dan Buettner visited some of the world's longest-living communities to discover the secrets of longevity. He went to Okinawa, where people live longer and healthier lives than anywhere else in the world.

Dan: They live about 22 percent longer than Americans. They have about four times as many 100-year-olds than we do.

Narrator: Buettner found that centenarians' lifestyles were similar, even if their cultures were different.

They tend to stay active and eat locally grown food. They have hobbies, like this Okinawan woman who works in her garden every day. Most centenarians also have access to good medical care . . . and they have the support of their friends and family.

These centenarians seem to be very healthy . . . but how much longer will such healthy lifestyles last? Younger people are eating more processed foods, and may be less active than their parents and grandparents. With increasing globalization, these traditional lifestyles are fast disappearing.

People today are turning to medical science to help live longer lives. Some scientists have started to treat aging as a disease instead of a natural part of human life.

For now though, there are few centenarians, like this 102-year-old, in the world. However, if we follow their example—eat healthy, stay active, and keep our families close—then we may see more centenarians in our future. And our future may be very long indeed.

Solar Cooking

UNIT 2

Narrator: It's a cold day in Borrego Springs, California, but Eleanor Shimeall is cooking outside. But she's not using electricity, gas, or any of the fuels we normally use in the kitchen.

Eleanor: I'm gonna check on this chicken and rice and see whether it's cooking. Ah, it's doing a good job.

Narrator: Instead, Eleanor is using the sun to make her meal. She has done this almost every day for the last 23 years. With sunshine, solar stoves can be used to cook everything from meat and fish, to bread and vegetables. This method is becoming popular with people who care about the environment.

Solar stoves can help save energy at home, and save lives in the developing world.

Dr. Metcalf: With sunshine, you have an alternative to fire. And that's important for two and a half billion people to learn about because they're running out of traditional fuels.

Narrator: Dr. Bob Metcalf is one of the people who started Solar Cookers International, a small group in Sacramento, California. SCI has taught people about solar cooking for the last 15 years, especially in the poor areas of Africa where people cannot afford a normal stove. They hope this innovation will also benefit women.

Dr. Metcalf: They have to walk about two to three miles or so to collect wood. And then they have to tend the fire, and the smoke from that fire—it burns their eyes and chokes their lungs.

Narrator: According to the World Health Organization, this pollution leads to the deaths of two million women and children each year.

With help from other groups, SCI has already trained more than 22,000 families to cook with the sun.

Woman #1: Oh, this is good. It's very good. The consistency is good, the texture is fine— no problem.

Woman #2: We're all amazed that a cardboard box can cook.

Narrator: People get their own solar stove to take home after each training. The stove costs about five dollars, lasts almost two years, and works just like the more expensive models.

Dr. Metcalf: Shiny things direct the sunshine onto a dark pot that then absorbs the sunshine, and changes that light energy into heat energy. And heat energy doesn't get out of the clear plastic bag, it doesn't get out of the window.

Narrator: There are also indications that solar cooking can help purify water.

About 6,000 people die every day from drinking dirty water. A solar cooker can heat water to a temperature that makes it safe to drink, and so preventing many deaths in developing countries.

From Nepal to Nicaragua, there are similar solar projects happening across the world. Some are even using much larger equipment, like this huge pizza cooker in Cuba.

But SCI hopes more communities will eventually use solar stoves. These efficient cookers have the power to help two and a half billion people. And maybe such creative yet simple solutions could lead to more devices powered by the sun.

Woman: OK, solar cooker!

UNIT 3 Lamu: Tradition and Modernity

Narrator: Lamu in Kenya, Africa, is a unique place. Stepping onto this island is like stepping back in time. Evidence of the past remains . . . along with old ways of doing things.

Lamu is the oldest town in Kenya, and the place where Swahili culture was born. On its old and very narrow streets, one of the most popular ways to get around is by donkey.

In 2001, Lamu town was placed on the United Nations list of World Heritage Sites. Many of the buildings are hundreds of years old. The most obvious influence is Arabic, but Lamu and its people absorb whatever cultures they come in contact with.

Badawy: Karibou, welcome.

Narrator: Sheik Ahmad Badawy's family has lived here for a few hundred years.

Badawy: Lamu is the cradle of Swahili civilization. This is where everybody depends on learning about the Swahili culture.

Narrator: It's a culture built on trade. Lamu was a busy economic center from as far back as the 14th century. Ships from China, India, Arabia, and Portugal sailed in and out, trading wood, spices, and many other goods. These traders all left a bit of themselves behind.

Badawy: That's how the culture is developed. Culture is dynamic. You blend in and when you blend in, it still retains the features of the Swahili people.

Narrator: These old interactions can be seen in faces on the street. But trading has decreased greatly in modern times, and the economy of Lamu has not grown. Community worker Amina Soud sees potential in the island's people.

Amina: We are trying to reach the people with the things they are used to, they are accustomed to. So when you go with it, they will just listen as it is and in the process, they will get the message that we want them to get.

Narrator: The message is that Lamu doesn't want to stay in the past. The hope—that people here will participate in the world beyond their island. Sheik Badawy, who owns an Internet café, wants this, too.

Badawy: You don't make money out of that . . . not really make money. But you connect and bring about what we call the tools that are needed to be with the world.

Narrator: But the relationship between modern and traditional is uneasy. Can Lamu change without losing its culture?

Badawy: Would you like to see it changed?

I don't think so. It's noise-free. So that the only noise you can get is from the microphone of the mosque, which is something sweet, I think.

Narrator: As Lamu looks to the future, its people also want to retain a strong connection with their past.

Amina: It is every day. I am telling you it is part of our life, it is our identity.

Saving Bluefin Tuna

Narrator: Japanese scientist Shukei Masuma is on a mission. He is trying to save the bluefin tuna from becoming extinct. Their numbers have declined significantly over the last decade, largely due to overfishing.

Masuma's solution? To breed them in captivity. He feeds the tuna himself. Here, he visits the huge pools where adults are separated from the young. Says Masuma: "I'm realizing more and more how difficult it is to uncover knowledge about the bluefin. At this point, I'm relying on all my strength and energy."

When evening comes, he waits at the edge of the pool. He hopes to see the beginning of bluefin life. Once the big fish have laid their eggs, Masuma slowly puts the eggs into special tanks. From this stage on, he will take care of them. His goal is to keep them alive until they are old enough to be returned to the sea. He hopes his tuna will grow large enough to breed in the wild.

It's a difficult job. Many hatchlings, or baby fish, do not survive. But after years of hard work, Masuma has found a stable temperature and the right food for his hatchlings. Now he is able to breed them in large numbers. He shows ocean scientist Sylvia Earle how life begins for these giant fish

Sylvia: Already you see the eyes. Is that what these are—the eyes beginning to form?

Masuma: Eyes, they have formed . . . and heart is beating, of course.

Sylvia: Masuma, you were the first to actually pull off this great miracle.

Masuma: Thank you very much.

Narrator: Someday, Masuma will send these hatchlings back into the ocean. There, they will hopefully have a positive effect on the population. But first they have to avoid getting caught.

Scientists estimate that the bluefin tuna population in the Atlantic Ocean is now only one-fifth of its population in the 1970s. And their numbers have dramatically decreased in the Mediterranean Sea and the Pacific Ocean.

The future for the species does not look good. Unless we greatly reduce the number of fish we catch each year, these giants of the sea will eventually die out.

Memory School

Narrator: London's taxi drivers are the Olympic athletes of memory. Drivers navigate the streets of London using a complex mental map with thousands of landmarks and other locations. These taxi drivers have helped researchers at University of London study how memory works.

Each new cab driver must pass a very difficult exam called "the knowledge," which takes about two years to prepare for. It's a good opportunity for scientists to study how the brain is able to adapt when it has to retain large amounts of information.

Passenger: Thanks, mate. Can you take me to Albert Hall?

Barry: When somebody gets in your cab, they'll say, "Take me to so-and-so." It's got to be like that . . . you've got to know instantly where you're going, which way to be pointing. So there's a lot of retention, you've got to retain a lot of what you've learned as well.

Narrator: Scientists suspected that a part of the brain called the hippocampus might be the key to the taxi drivers' success.

Teacher: Matt, now run me to the nearest police station.

Student: Leave by Waterloo Bridge, forward Lancaster Place . . .

Narrator: Drivers-in-training at the Knowledge Point School use this part of the brain a lot in classes.

Teacher: Dave, give me the name of a restaurant on Portland Road with a lady's name.

Student: Chutney Mary's.

Teacher: Hereford Road—where would you give me?

Student: Veronica's.

Narrator: After class, students take their knowledge to the streets. Visual processing takes up more space in the brain than all the other senses combined. So direct experience is a very important part of training.

James: You start off learning all the roads. Then you have to learn all the places on every road. With all the routes that you have to do for the knowledge, you couldn't possibly do it on a map. You have to get out on your bike, in the rain, the cold, the snow. You learn it bit by bit.

Narrator: But how does the brain retain and order all that information? All this internal effort has an external effect—a physical change in the brain itself.

From their study, scientists concluded that taxi drivers have a larger hippocampus than the average person. In fact, the biggest differences were seen in taxi drivers who had been working a long time.

Andy: It's almost like you've somehow, somewhere up in your brain, you've created enough space to sort of slip this map in, a little bit of software.

Narrator: This study suggests that the adult brain can physically change depending on what a person needs. Doctors hope this information can be used to help restore the minds of stroke victims, Alzheimer's patients, and those suffering other forms of brain damage.

Contents

Tips for Reading and Note Taking

Tips for Writing and Research

Tips for Reading and Note Taking

Reading fluently

Why develop your reading speed?

Reading slowly, one word at a time, makes it difficult to get an overall sense of the meaning of a text. As a result, reading becomes more challenging and less interesting than if you read at a faster pace. In general, it is a good idea to first skim a text for the gist, and then read it again more closely so that you can focus on the most relevant details.

Strategies for improving reading speed:

- Try to read groups of words rather than individual words.
- Keep your eyes moving forward. Read through to the end of each sentence or paragraph instead of going back to reread words or phrases within the sentence or paragraph.
- Read selectively. Skip functional words (articles, prepositions, etc.) and focus on words and phrases carrying meaning—the content words. See page 48 for an example.
- Use clues in the text—such as highlighted text (**bold** words, words in *italics*, etc.)—to help you know which parts might be important and worth focusing on.
- Use section headings, as well as the first and last lines of paragraphs, to help you understand how the text is organized.
- Use context and other clues such as affixes and part of speech to guess the meaning of unfamiliar words and phrases. Try to avoid using a dictionary if you are reading quickly for overall meaning.

Thinking critically

As you read, ask yourself questions about what the writer is saying, and how and why the writer is presenting the information at hand.

Important critical thinking skills for academic reading and writing:

- Analyzing: Examining a text in close detail in order to identify key points, similarities, and differences.
- Evaluating: Using evidence to decide how relevant, important, or useful something is. This often involves looking at reasons for and against something.
- Inferring: "Reading between the lines;" in other words, identifying what a writer is saying indirectly, or *implicitly*, rather than directly, or *explicitly*.
- Synthesizing: Gathering appropriate information and ideas from more than one source and making a judgment, summary, or conclusion based on the evidence.
- Reflecting: Relating ideas and information in a text to your own personal experience and preconceptions (i.e., the opinions or beliefs you had before reading the text).

Note taking

Taking notes of key points and the connections between them will help you better understand the overall meaning and organization of a text. Note taking also enables you to record the most important ideas and information for future use such as when you are preparing for an exam or completing a writing assignment.

Techniques for effective note taking:

- As you read, underline or highlight important information such as dates, names, places, and other facts.
- Take notes in the margin—as you read, note the main idea and supporting details next to each paragraph. Also note your own ideas or questions about the paragraph.
- On paper or on a computer, paraphrase the key points of the text in your own words.
- Keep your notes brief—include short headings to organize the information, key words and phrases (not full sentences), and abbreviations and symbols. (See next page for examples.)
- Note sources of information precisely. Be sure to include page numbers, names of relevant people and places, and quotations.
- Make connections between key points with techniques such as using arrows and colors to connect ideas and drawing circles or squares around related information.
- Use a graphic organizer to summarize a text, particularly if it follows a pattern such as cause—effect, comparison—contrast, or chronological sequence.
- Use your notes to write a summary of the passage in order to remember what you learned.

Useful abbreviations

approx.	approximately	incl.	including
ca.	about, around (date / year)	info	information
cd	could	p. (pp.)	page (pages)
Ch.	Chapter	para.	paragraph
devt	development	re:	regarding, concerning
e.g./ex.	example	wd	would
etc.	and others / and the rest	yr(s)	years(s)
excl.	excluding	C20	20th century
govt	government		
i.e.	that is; in other words		
impt	important		

Useful symbols

→	leads to / causes
↑	increases / increased
↓	decreases / decreased
& or +	and
∴	therefore
b/c	because
w/	with
=	is the same as
>	is more than
<	is less than
~	is approximately / about

Learning vocabulary

More than likely, you will not remember a new word or phrase after reading or hearing it once. You need to use the word several times before it enters your long-term memory.

Strategies for learning vocabulary:

- Use flash cards. Write the words you want to learn on one side of an index card. Write the definition and/or an example sentence that uses the word on the other side. Use your flash cards to test your knowledge of new vocabulary.
- Keep a vocabulary journal. When you come across a new word or phrase, write a short definition of the word (in English, if possible) and the sentence or situation where you found it (its context). Write another sentence of your own that uses the word. Include any common collocations. (See the Word Partners boxes in this book for examples of collocations.)
- Make word webs (or "word maps").
- Use memory aids. It may be easier to remember a word or phrase if you use a memory aid, or *mnemonic*. For example, if you want to learn the idiom *keep an eye on someone*, which means to "watch someone carefully," you might picture yourself putting your eyeball on someone's shoulder so that you can watch the person carefully. The stranger the picture is, the more you will remember it! See page 88 for more on mnemonics.

Common affixes

Some words contain an affix at the start of the word (*prefix*) and/or at the end (*suffix*). These affixes can be useful for guessing the meaning of unfamiliar words and for expanding your vocabulary. In general, a prefix affects the meaning of a word, whereas a suffix affects its part of speech. See the Word Link boxes in this book for specific examples.

Prefix	Meaning	Example
commun-	sharing	communicate
con-	together, with	construct
em- / en-	making, putting	empower, endanger
ex-	away, from, out	external
in-	not	independent
inter-	between	interactive
minim-	smallest	minimal
pre-	before	prevent
re-	back, again	restore
sur	above	surface
trans-	across	transfer
un-	not	uninvolved

Suffix	Part of Speech	Example
-able	adjective	dependable
-al	adjective	traditional
-ate	verb	differentiate
-ed	adjective	involved
-eer	noun	volunteer
-ent / -ant	adjective	confident, significant
-er	noun	researcher
-ful	adjective	grateful
-ical	adjective	practical
-ity	noun	reality
-ive	adjective	positive
-ize	verb	socialize
-ly	adverb	definitely
-ment	noun	achievement
-tion	noun	prevention

Tips for Writing and Research

Features of academic writing

There are many types of academic writing (descriptive, argumentative/persuasive, narrative, etc.), but most types share similar characteristics.

Generally, in academic writing you should:

- write in full sentences.
- use formal English. (Avoid slang or conversational expressions such as *kind of*.)
- be clear and coherent—keep to your main point; avoid technical words that the reader may not know.
- use signal words and phrases to connect your ideas. (See examples on page 214.)
- have a clear point (main idea) for each paragraph.
- be objective—most academic writing uses a neutral, impersonal point of view, so avoid overuse of personal pronouns (*I, we, you*) and subjective language such as *nice* or *terrible*.
- use facts, examples, and expert opinions to support your argument.
- show where the evidence or opinions come from. (*According to the 2009 World Database Survey,. . . .*)
- show that you have considered other viewpoints.

Generally, in academic writing you should <u>not</u>:

- use abbreviations or language used in texting. (Use *that is* rather than *i.e.*, and *in my opinion*, not *IMO*.)
- use contractions. (Use *is not* rather than *isn't*.)
- be vague. (*A man made the first cell-phone call a few decades ago.* -> *An inventor named Martin Cooper made the first cell-phone call in 1973.*)
- include several pronoun references in a single sentence. (*He thinks it's a better idea than the other one, but I agree with her.*)
- start sentences with *or, and,* or *but*.
- apologize to the reader. (*I'm sorry I don't know much about this, but . . .*) In academic writing, it is important to sound confident about what you are saying!

Proofreading tips

Capitalization

Remember to capitalize:

- the first letter of the word at the beginning of every sentence.
- proper names such as names of people, geographical names, company names, and names of organizations.
- days, months, and holidays.
- the word *I*.
- the first letter of a title such as the title of a movie or a book.
- the words in titles that have meaning (content words). Don't capitalize *a, an, the, and,* or prepositions such as *to, for, of, from, at, in,* and *on*, unless they are the first word of a title (e.g., *The King and I*).

Punctuation

Keep the following rules in mind:

- Use a question mark (?) at the end of every question. Use a period (.) at the end of any sentence that is not a question.
- Exclamation marks (!), which indicate strong feelings such as surprise or joy, are generally not used in academic writing.
- Use commas (,) to separate a list of three or more things (*She speaks German, English, and Spanish.*).
- Use a comma after an introductory word or phrase. (*Although painful to humans, it is not deadly. / However, some species have fewer than 20 legs.*)
- Use a comma before a combining word (coordinating conjunction)—*and, but, so, yet, or,* and *nor*—that joins two sentences (*Black widow bites are not usually deadly for adults, but they can be deadly for children.*).
- Use an apostrophe (') for showing possession (*James's idea came from social networking sites.*).

- Use quotation marks (" ") to indicate the exact words used by someone else. (*In fact, Wesch says, "the Web is us."*)
- Use quotation marks to show when a word or phrase is being used in a special way, such as a definition. (*The name centipede means "100 legs."*)

Other Proofreading Tips:

- Print out your draft instead of reading it on your computer screen.
- Read your draft out loud. Use your finger or a pen to point to each word as you read it.
- Don't be afraid to mark up your draft. Use a colored pen to make corrections so you can see them easily when you write your next draft.
- Read your draft backwards—starting with the last word—to check your spelling. That way, you won't be distracted by the meaning.
- Have someone else read your draft and give you comments or ask you questions.
- Don't depend on a computer's spell-check. When the spell-check suggests a correction, make sure you agree with it before you accept the change.
- Remember to pay attention to the following items:
  - Short words such as *is*, *and*, *but*, *or*, *it*, *to*, *for*, *from*, and *so*.
  - Spelling of proper nouns.
  - Numbers and dates.
- Keep a list of spelling and grammar mistakes that you commonly make so that you can be aware of them as you edit your draft.

Watch out for frequently confused words:

- *there, their,* and *they're*
- *its* and *it's*
- *by, buy,* and *bye*
- *your* and *you're*
- *to, too,* and *two*
- *whose* and *who's*
- *where, wear, we're,* and *were*
- *then* and *than*
- *quit, quiet,* and *quite*
- *write* and *right*
- *affect* and *effect*
- *through* and *threw*
- *week* and *weak*

Research and referencing

Using facts and expert quotes from journals and online sources will help to support your arguments in a written assignment. When you research information, you need to look for the most relevant and reliable sources. You will also need to provide appropriate citations for these sources; that is, you need to indicate that the words are not your own but rather come from someone else.

In academic writing, it is necessary for a writer to cite sources of all information that is not original. Using a source without citing it is known as **plagiarism**.

There are several ways to cite sources. Check with your teacher on the method or methods required at your institution.

Research Checklist

☐ Are my sources relevant to the assignment?

☐ Are my sources reliable? Think about the author and publisher. Ask yourself, "What is the author's point of view? Can I trust this information?"

☐ Have I noted all sources properly, including page numbers?

☐ When I am not citing a source directly, am I using my own words? In other words, am I using appropriate paraphrasing, which includes the use of synonyms, different word forms, and/or different grammatical structure?

☐ Are my sources up-to-date? Do they use the most recent data available? Having current sources is especially important for fields that change rapidly, such as technology and business.

☐ If I am using a direct quote, am I using the exact words that the person said or wrote?

☐ Am I using varied expressions for introducing citations, such as *According to X, As X says, X says / states / points out / explains . . .*?

Common signal phrases

Making an overview statement

It is generally agreed that . . .
It is clear (from the chart/table) that . . .
Generally, we can see that . . .

Giving supporting details and examples

One/An example (of this) is. . .
For example,. . . / For instance, . . .
Specifically, . . . / More specifically, . . .
From my experience, . . .

Giving reasons

This is due to . . .
This is because (of) . . .
One reason (for this) is . . .

Describing cause and effect

Consequently, . . . / Therefore, . . .
As a result, . . . /
As a consequence, . . .

This means that . . .
Because of this, . . .

Giving definitions

. . . which means . . .
In other words,. . .
That is . . .

Linking arguments and reasons

Furthermore, . . . / Moreover, . . .
In addition, . . . / Additionally, . . .
For one thing, . . . / For another example, . . .
Not only . . . but also . . .

Describing a process

First (of all), . . .
Then / Next / After that, . . .
As soon as . . . / When . . .
Finally, . . .

Outlining contrasting views

On the other hand, . . . / However, . . .
Although some people believe (that) . .
it can also be argued that . . .
While it may be true that . . .,
nevertheless, . . .
Despite this, . . . / Despite
(the fact that) . . . Even though . . .

Softening a statement

It seems/appears that . . .
The evidence suggests/indicates that . . .

Giving a personal opinion

In my opinion, . . .
I (generally) agree that . . .
I think/feel that . . .
Personally, I believe (that) . . .

Restating/concluding

In conclusion, . . . / In summary, . . .
To conclude, . . . / To summarize, . . .

Grammar Reference

Unit 1

Language for Writing: Review of the Simple Present

Affirmative and Negative Statements				
Affirmative Statements		**Negative Statements**		
Subject	**Verb**	**Subject**	***Do/Does Not***	**Verb (Base Form)**
I You We They	**live** in Singapore.	I You We They	**do not** **don't**	**live** in Mexico.
He She It	**lives** in Singapore.	He She It	**does not** **doesn't**	

Affirmative and Negative Statements with *Be*					
Affirmative Statements			**Negative Statements**		
Subject	***Am/Are/Is***		**Subject**	***Am/Are/Is***	
I	**am**	happy. here. at work.	I	**am not**	happy. here. at work.
You We They	**are**		You We They	**are not** **aren't**	
He She It	**is**		He She It	**is not** **isn't**	

Unit 2

Language for Writing: Review of the Simple Past

Affirmative and Negative Statements

Affirmative Statements		Negative Statements		
Subject	**Verb (Past Form)**	**Subject**	***Did Not***	**Verb (Base Form)**
I You We They He She It	**started** a project. **walked** home. **studied**. **went** to school.	I You We They He She It	**did not** **didn't**	**start** a project. **walk** home. **study**. **go** to school.

Spelling Rules for Regular Verbs

1. Add *-ed* to most verbs. 2. If a one-syllable verb ends in *e*, add *-d*. 3. If a one-syllable verb ends in a consonant + vowel + consonant (not *w*, *x*, or *y*), double the consonant and add *-ed*. 4. If a two-syllable word ends in consonant + vowel + consonant, double the last consonant only if the stress is on the last syllable. 5. If a verb ends in consonant + *-y*, drop the *-y* and add *-ied*	talk—talked like—liked stop—stopped prefer—preferred edit—edited study—studied

Past Forms of Commonly Used Irregular Verbs

become—became begin—began build—built break—broke bring—brought buy—bought choose—chose come—came do—did draw—drew eat—ate	fall—fell find—found forget—forgot get—got give—gave go—went have—had hear—heard know—knew lose—lost make—made	read—read say—said see—saw speak—spoke spend—spent take—took teach—taught tell—told think—thought understand—understood write—wrote

Affirmative and Negative Statements with *Be*

Affirmative Statements			Negative Statements		
Subject	***Was/Were***		**Subject**	***Was/Were Not***	
I He She It	**was**	happy. sad. a doctor. a student. here. at work.	I He She It	**was not** **wasn't**	happy. sad. a doctor. a student. here. at work.
You We They	**were**		You We They	**were not** **weren't**	

Unit 3

The Present Perfect

Subject	*Have/Have Not*	Verb (Past Participle)	Time Marker (optional)
I You We They	**have** **have not / haven't**	**been** here **seen** her **called** him	since last year. for three months. recently.
He She It	**has** **has not / hasn't**		

Time Markers

Use *since* + a point in time, *for* + a length of time, *in the* + time period to describe something that began in the past and continues to the present.

I've lived in Denmark **since** 2010.
He hasn't been here **for** three years.
We've met a lot of people **in the past month**.

Use *already* in affirmative statements to emphasize that something happened at an unspecified time in the past. Use *yet* in negative statements to talk about something that has not happened before now.

I've seen that movie **already**.
She's **already** eaten.

I haven't seen that movie **yet**.
She hasn't eaten **yet**.

Use words such as *a few times*, *twice*, or a number to describe something that happened more than once in the past.

We've been to Mexico a **few times**.
Mark has called **twice**.
They've sent us **five** emails.

Use *recently* or *lately* to emphasize that something happened or didn't happen at an unspecified time in the recent past.

Sarah has called several times **recently**.
I haven't seen James **lately**.

Past Participle Forms of Commonly Used Irregular Verbs

be—been	find—found	say—said
become—become	forget—forgotten	see—seen
begin—begun	get—gotten	show—shown
build—built	give—given	sing—sung
break—broken	go—gone	sleep—slept
bring—brought	have—had	speak—spoken
buy—bought	hear—heard	spend—spent
choose—chosen	know—known	take—taken
come—come	lose—lost	teach—taught
do—done	make—made	tell—told
draw—drawn	meet—met	think—thought
eat—eaten	put—put	understand—understood
fall—fallen	read—read	write—written

Unit 5

Spelling Rules for Forming Gerunds

When forming gerunds, follow these rules for adding -ing to verbs:

1. Most verbs: add -ing:
   sleep → sleeping   think → thinking   remember → remembering

2. Verbs that end with a consonant followed by -e: drop the -e and add -ing:
   memorize → memorizing   store → storing   use → using

3. One-syllable verbs ending with a consonant + vowel + consonant: double the final consonant and add -ing:
   get → getting   stop → stopping   put → putting
   (Exceptions: Verbs that end in -w, -x, or -y; for example, say → saying)

4. Two-syllable verbs ending with a consonant + vowel + consonant, where the second syllable is stressed: double the final consonant and add -ing:
   admit → admitting   begin → beginning   prefer → preferring

Vocabulary Index

*These words are on the Academic Word List (AWL). The AWL is a list of the 570 most frequent word families in academic texts. The list does not include words that are among the most frequent 2,000 words of English. For more information on the AWL, see http://www.victoria.ac.nz/lals/resources/academicwordlist/.

Critical Thinking

Analyzing 7, 18, 28, 38, 56, 58, 67, 74, 75, 76, 78, 88, 95, 96, 98

Applying a Method 87

Brainstorming 4, 9, 11, 15, 24, 29, 44, 49, 55, 64, 69, 71, 75, 89, 95

Evaluating 67

Guessing meaning from context 7, 9, 49, 67, 89

Making connections/comparisons 2, 42, 27

Making inferences 47, 54, 87

Peer-Evaluating 97

Personalizing/Reflecting 1, 21, 22, 41, 61, 81

Predicting 4, 24, 31, 44, 51, 64, 71, 84, 91

Ranking and justifying 22, 34

Synthesizing 9, 14, 29, 34, 49, 68, 69, 74, 89, 94

Grammar

By + gerund 95, 99

Present perfect tense 55, 59

Simple past tense 35, 39

Simple present tense 15, 19

Reading Skills/Strategies

Identifying:

cause and effect 88, 94

key details 7, 14, 27, 34, 47, 54, 74, 87, 94

main idea 8, 54, 67, 94

purpose 74

supporting ideas/details 28, 34, 36

Understanding the gist 7, 14, 27, 34, 47, 48, 54, 67, 74, 87, 94

Visual Literacy

Interpreting graphic information

- graphs/charts 68, 75, 76, 78, 83, 93

- infographics 42, 73

- maps 42, 62, 68

Using graphic organizers

- T-charts 84, 87

- mind maps 11

Vocabulary Skills

Building vocabulary 4, 10, 24, 30, 44, 50, 64, 70, 84, 90

Using a dictionary 69

Using vocabulary 4, 11, 24, 31, 44, 51, 64, 71, 84, 91

Word Link 4, 24, 30, 44, 50, 70, 84, 91

Word Partners 10, 50, 64, 70, 90

Writing Skills

Describing and explaining charts and graphs 75, 76

Drafting 17, 37, 57, 77, 96, 97

Editing 19, 20, 39, 40, 59, 60, 79, 80, 99, 100

Journal writing 15, 36, 55, 75, 95

Revising 18, 38, 58, 78

Supporting the main idea and giving details 36

Writing a concluding sentence 56

Writing a topic sentence 16

Academic Literacy Skills Index

Test-Taking Skills

The authors and publisher would like to thank the following reviewers for their help during the development of this series:

UNITED STATES AND CANADA

Gokhan Alkanat, Auburn University at Montgomery, AL; Nikki Ashcraft, Shenandoah University, VA; Karin Avila-John, University of Dayton, OH; John Baker, Oakland Community College, MI; Shirley Baker, Alliant International University, CA; Michelle Bell, University of South Florida, FL; Nancy Boyer, Golden West College, CA; Kathy Brenner, BU/CELOP, Mattapan, MA; Janna Brink, Mt. San Antonio College, Chino Hills, CA; Carol Brutza, Gateway Community College, CT; Sarah Camp, University of Kentucky, Center for ESL, KY; Maria Caratini, Eastfield College, TX; Ana Maria Cepero, Miami Dade College, Miami, FL; Daniel Chaboya, Tulsa Community College, OK; Patricia Chukwueke, English Language Institute – UCSD Extension, CA; Julia A. Correia, Henderson State University, CT; Suzanne Crisci, Bunker Hill Community College, MA; Lina Crocker, University of Kentucky, Lexington, KY; Katie Crowder, University of North Texas, TX; Joe Cunningham, Park University, Kansas City, MO; Lynda Dalgish, Concordia College, NY; Jeffrey Diluglio, Center for English Language and Orientation Programs: Boston University, MA; Scott Dirks, Kaplan International Center at Harvard Square, MA; Kathleen Dixon, SUNY Stony Brook - Intensive English Center, Stony Brook, NY; Margo Downey, Boston University, Boston, MA; John Drezek, Richland College, TX; Qian Du, Ohio State University, Columbus, OH; Leslie Kosel Eckstein, Hillsborough Community College, FL; Anwar El-Issa, Antelope Valley College, CA; Beth Kozbial Ernst, University of Wisconsin-Eau Claire, WI; Anrisa Fannin, The International Education Center at Diablo Valley College, CA; Jennie Farnell, Greenwich Japanese School, Greenwich, CT; Rosa Vasquez Fernandez, John F. Kennedy, Institute Of Languages, Inc., Boston, MA; Mark Fisher, Lone Star College, TX; Celeste Flowers, University of Central Arkansas, AR; John Fox, English Language Institute, GA; Pradel R. Frank, Miami Dade College, FL; Sherri Fujita, Hawaii Community College, Hilo, HI; Sally Gearheart, Santa Rosa Jr. College, CA; Elizabeth Gillstrom, The University of Pennsylvania, Philadelphia, PA; Sheila Goldstein, Rockland Community College, Brentwood, NY; Karen Grubbs, ELS Language Centers, FL; Sudeepa Gulati, long beach city college, Torrance, CA; Joni Hagigeorges, Salem State University, MA; Marcia Peoples Halio, English Language Institute, University of Delaware, DE; Kara Hanson, Oregon State University, Corvallis, OR; Suha Hattab, Triton College, Chicago, IL; Marla Heath, Sacred Heart Univiversity and Norwalk Community College, Stamford, CT; Valerie Heming, University of Central Missouri, MO; Mary Hill, North Shore Community College, MA; Harry Holden, North Lake College, Dallas, TX; Ingrid Holm, University of Massachusetts Amherst, MA; Katie Hurter, Lone Star College – North Harris, TX; Barbara Inerfeld, Program in American Language Studies (PALS) Rutgers University/New Brunswick, Piscataway, NJ; Justin Jernigan, Georgia Gwinnett College, GA; Barbara Jonckheere, ALI/CSULB, Long Beach, CA; Susan Jordan, Fisher College, MA; Maria Kasparova, Bergen Community College, NJ; Maureen Kelbert, Vancouver Community College, Surrey, BC, Canada; Gail Kellersberger, University of Houston-Downtown, TX; David Kent, Troy University, Goshen,

AL; Daryl Kinney, Los Angeles City College, CA; Jennifer Lacroix, Center for English Language and Orientation Programs: Boston University, MA; Stuart Landers, Misouri State University, Springfield, MO; Mary Jo Fletcher LaRocco, Ph.D., Salve Regina University, Newport, RI; Bea Lawn, Gavilan College, Gilroy, CA; Margaret V. Layton, University of Nevada, Reno Intensive English Language Center, NV; Alice Lee, Richland College, Mesquite, TX; Heidi Lieb, Bergen Community College, NJ; Kerry Linder, Language Studies International New York, NY; Jenifer Lucas-Uygun, Passaic County Community College, Paterson, NJ; Alison MacAdams, Approach International Student Center, MA; Julia MacDonald, Brock University, Saint Catharines, ON, Canada; Craig Machado, Norwalk Community College, CT; Andrew J. MacNeill, Southwestern College, CA; Melanie A. Majeski, Naugatuck Valley Community College, CT; Wendy Maloney, College of DuPage, Aurora, IL; Chris Mares, University of Maine – Intensive English Institute, Maine; Josefina Mark, Union County College, NJ; Connie Mathews, Nashville State Community College, TN; Bette Matthews, Mid-Pacific Institute, HI; Richard McDorman, inlingua Language Centers (Miami, FL) and Pennsylvania State University, Pompano Beach, FL; Sara McKinnon, College of Marin, CA; Christine Mekkaoui, Pittsburg State University, KS; Holly A. Milkowart, Johnson County Community College, KS; Donna Moore, Hawaii Community College, Hilo, HI; Ruth W. Moore, International English Center, University of Colorado at Boulder, CO; Kimberly McGrath Moreira, University of Miami, FL; Warren Mosher, University of Miami, FL; Sarah Moyer, California State University Long Beach, CA; Lukas Murphy, Westchester Community College, NY; Elena Nehrebecki, Hudson Community College, NJ; Bjarne Nielsen, Central Piedmont Community College, North Carolina; David Nippoldt, Reedley College, CA; Nancy Nystrom, University Of Texas At San Antonio, Austin, TX; Jane O'Connor, Emory College, Atlanta, GA; Daniel E. Opacki, SIT Graduate Institute, Brattleboro, VT; Lucia Parsley, Virginia Commonwealth University, VA; Wendy Patriquin, Parkland College, IL; Nancy Pendleton, Cape Cod Community College, Attleboro, MA; Marion Piccolomini, Communicate With Ease, LTD, PA; Barbara Pijan, Portland State University, Portland, OR; Marjorie Pitts, Ohio Northern University, Ada, OH; Carolyn Prager, Spanish-American Institute, NY; Eileen Prince, Prince Language Associates Incorporated, MA; Sema Pulak, Texas A & M University, TX; Mary Kay Purcell, University of Evansville, Evansville, IN; Christina Quartararo, St. John's University, Jamaica, NY; James T. Raby, Clark University, MA; Anouchka Rachelson, Miami-Dade College, FL; Sherry Rasmussen, DePaul University, IL; Amy Renehan, University of Washington, WA; Daniel Rivas, Irvine Valley College, Irvine, CA; Esther Robbins, Prince George's Community College, PA; Bruce Rogers, Spring International Language Center at Arapahoe College, Littleton, CO; Helen Roland, Miami Dade College, FL; Linda Roth, Vanderbilt University English Language Center, TN; Janine Rudnick, El Paso Community College, TX; Paula Sanchez, Miami Dade College – Kendall Campus, FL; Deborah Sandstrom, Tutorium in Intensive English at University of Illinois at Chicago, Elmhurst, IL; Marianne Hsu Santelli, Middlesex County College, NJ; Elena Sapp, INTO Oregon State University, Corvallis, OR; Alice Savage, Lone Star College System: North Harris, TX; Jitana Schaefer, Pensacola State College, Pensacola, FL; Lynn Ramage Schaefer, University of Central Arkansas, AR; Ann Schroth, Johnson & Wales University, Dayville, CT;

Acknowledgments

Margaret Shippey, Miami Dade College, FL; Lisa Sieg, Murray State University, KY; Samanthia Slaight, North Lake College, Richardson, TX; Ann Snider, UNK University of NE Kearney, Kearney, NE; Alison Stamps, ESL Center at Mississippi State University, Mississippi; Peggy Street, ELS Language Centers, Miami, FL; Lydia Streiter, York College Adult Learning Center, NY; Steve Strizver, Miami Beach, FL; Nicholas Taggart, Arkansas State University, AR; Marcia Takacs, Coastline Community College, CA; Tamara Teffeteller, University of California Los Angeles, American Language Center, CA; Adrianne Aiko Thompson, Miami Dade College, Miami, FL; Rebecca Toner, English Language Programs, University of Pennsylvania, PA; Evina Baquiran Torres, Zoni Language Centers, NY; William G. Trudeau, Missouri Southern State University, MO; Troy Tucker, Edison State College, FL; Maria Vargas-O'Neel, Miami Dade College, FL; Amerca Vazquez, Miami Dade College, FL; Alison Vinande, Modesto Junior College, CA; Christie Ward, IELP, Central CT State University, Hartford, CT; Colin Ward, Lone Star College - North Harris, Houston, TX; Denise Warner, Lansing Community College, Lansing, MI; Rita Rutkowski Weber, University of Wisconsin – Milwaukee, WI; James Wilson, Cosumnes River College, Sacramento, CA; Dolores "Lorrie" Winter, California State University Fullerton, Buena Park, CA; Wendy Wish-Bogue, Valencia Community College, FL; Cissy Wong, Sacramento City College, CA; Sarah Worthington, Tucson, Arizona; Kimberly Yoder, Kent State University, ESL Center, OH.

ASIA

Nor Azni Abdullah, Universiti Teknologi Mara; Morgan Bapst, Seoul National University of Science and Technology; Herman Bartelen, Kanda Institute of Foreign Languages, Sano; Maiko Berger, Ritsumeikan Asia Pacific University; Thomas E. Bieri, Nagoya College; Paul Bournhonesque, Seoul National University of Technology; Joyce Cheah Kim Sim, Taylor's University, Selangor Darul Ehsan; Michael C. Cheng, National Chengchi University; Fu-Dong Chiou, National Taiwan University; Derek Currie, Korea University, Sejong Institute of Foreign Language Studies; Wendy Gough, St. Mary College/Nunoike Gaigo Senmon Gakko, Ichinomiya; Christoph A. Hafner, City University of Hong Kong; Monica Hamciuc, Ritsumeikan Asia-Pacific University, Kagoshima; Rob Higgens, Ritsumeikan University; Wenhua Hsu, I-Shou University; Helen Huntley, Hanoi University; Debra Jones, Tokyo Woman's Christian University, Tokyo; Shih Fan Kao, JinWen University of Science and Technology; Ikuko Kashiwabara, Osaka Electro-Communication University; Alyssa Kim, Hankuk University of Foreign Studies; Richard S. Lavin, Prefecturla University of Kumamoto; Mike Lay, American Institute Cambodia; Byoung-Kyo Lee, Yonsei University; Lin Li, Capital Normal University, Beijing; Bien Thi Thanh Mai, The International University – Vietnam National University, Ho Chi Minh City; Hudson Murrell, Baiko Gakuin University; Keiichi Narita, Niigata University; Orapin Nasawang, Udon Thani Rajabhat University; Huynh Thi Ai Nguyen, Vietnam USA Society; James Pham, IDP Phnom Penh; John Racine, Dokkyo University; Duncan Rose, British Council Singapore; Greg Rouault, Konan University, Hirao School of Management, Osaka; Simone Samuels, The Indonesia Australia Language Foundation, Jakarta; Yuko Shimizu, Ritsumeikan University; Wang Songmei, Beijing Institute of Education Faculty; Richmond Stroupe, Soka University; Peechaya Suriyawong, Udon Thani Rajabhat

University; Teoh Swee Ai, Universiti Teknologi Mara; Chien-Wen Jenny Tseng, National Sun Yat-Sen University; Hajime Uematsu, Hirosaki University; Sy Vanna, Newton Thilay School, Phnom Penh; Matthew Watterson, Hongik University; Anthony Zak, English Language Center, Shantou University.

LATIN AMERICA AND THE CARIBBEAN

Ramon Aguilar, Universidad Tecnológica de Hermosillo, México; Lívia de Araújo Donnini Rodrigues, University of São Paolo, Brazil; Cecilia Avila, Universidad de Xapala, México; Beth Bartlett, Centro Cultural Colombo Americano, Cali, Colombia; Raúl Billini, Colegio Loyola, Dominican Republic; Nohora Edith Bryan, Universidad de La Sabana, Colombia; Raquel Hernández Cantú, Instituto Tecnológico de Monterrey, Mexico; Millie Commander, Inter American University of Puerto Rico, Puerto Rico; José Alonso Gaxiola Soto, CEI Universidad Autonoma de Sinaloa, Mazatlán, Mexico; Raquel Hernandez, Tecnologico de Monterrey, Mexico; Edwin Marín-Arroyo, Instituto Tecnológico de Costa Rica; Rosario Mena, Instituto Cultural Dominico-Americano, Dominican Republic; Elizabeth Ortiz Lozada, COPEI-COPOL English Institute, Ecuador; Gilberto Rios Zamora, Sinaloa State Language Center, Mexico; Patricia Veciños, El Instituto Cultural Argentino Norteamericano, Argentina; Isabela Villas Boas, Casa Thomas Jefferson, Brasília, Brazil; Roxana Viñes, Language Two School of English, Argentina.

EUROPE, MIDDLE EAST, AND NORTH AFRICA

Tom Farkas, American University of Cairo, Egypt; Ghada Hozayen, Arab Academy for Science, Technology and Maritime Transport, Egypt; Tamara Jones, ESL Instructor, SHAPE Language Center, Belgium; Jodi Lefort, Sultan Qaboos University, Muscat, Oman; Neil McBeath, Sultan Qaboos University, Oman; Barbara R. Reimer, CERTESL, UAE University, UAE; Nashwa Nashaat Sobhy, The American University in Cairo, Egypt; Virginia Van Hest-Bastaki, Kuwait University, Kuwait.

AUSTRALIA

Susan Austin, University of South Australia, Joanne Cummins, Swinburne College; Pamela Humphreys, Griffith University.

Special thanks to Dan Buettner, Jane Chen, Barton Seaver, and James Vlahos for their kind assistance during this book's development.

This series is dedicated to Kristin L. Johannsen, whose love for the world's cultures and concern for the world's environment were an inspiration to family, friends, students, and colleagues.

Map and Illustration Images

2: National Geographic Maps; **5:** National Geographic Maps; **6:** National Geographic Maps; **12-13:** Illustrations Blue Zones LLC; **21:** Ken Eward/National Geographic Stock; **22-23:** Mr. Griff Wason/National Geographic Image Collection; **25:** Workshop Loves You; **25:** National Geographic Maps; **27:** Workshop Loves You; **42-43:** National Geographic Maps; **43:** Oliver Uberti/National Geographic Image Collection; **49:** National Geographic Maps; **52:** National Geographic Maps; **62-63:** Benjamin Halpern and others, National Center for Ecological Analysis and Synthesis, University of California, Santa Barbara; **66:** Martin Gamache/National Geographic Image Collection; **72-73:** Mariel Furlong/Alejandro Tumas/National Geographic Image Collection; **75:** Page2, LLC; **76:** Page2, LLC; **78:** Page2, LLC; **83:** Anne Keiser/National Geographic; **83:** Page2, LLC; **93:** National Geographic Maps; **100:** Syakobchuk Vasyl, 2009/ Used under license from Shutterstock.com